Successful Selling

By: Michael Alexander

Table of Contents

Prologue

There are thousands of books in the marketplace on the topic of Selling. Some are excellent and worth the read, but most teach outdated methods that do not work in today's business climate. The sales profession has been under tremendous pressure in the last few years to produce more results, but in today's economic environment we need to equip our sales teams with better knowledge and strategies in order for companies to succeed.

The purpose of this book is to help sales professionals and sales managers understand that successful selling is not complicated and that there are easy solutions to help achieve better results. We will show you how to develop simple selling strategies and utilize our unique motivational tips to keep you focused.

This book offers the reader an inside look at the skills and strategies used by the some of the world's most successful salespeople.

Chapter 1

B2B and B2C Selling

There are many types of selling but the core principles remain the same for all.

B2B Selling

B2B (Business to Business) or Commercial selling, is any product or service where the customer does not come to you at your place of business. The expectation of the salesperson is to go outside their company walls to pursue sales from other businesses.

The Process

Step 1: Know your target market

What many sales and business people fail to do is to clearly identify who their target market is. They feel that "everybody is a prospect". Even though your product may very well be usable by "everybody" or every company, not everybody has the ability to make the buying decision. So, in order to create a successful selling environment, you must know the demographics of your decision maker(s).

In B2B selling is the final decision made at the C-Level (CEO, COO, etc...)? Vice President? Human Resources? Purchasing Manager? Is there only one decision maker, or are there multiple?

If multiple, what specific benefits will each one look for from your product or service?

In B2C selling is the final decision made by the person in front of you, their spouse, their friend or their children?

Just remember that for every buying decision there are **four buying roles** that will be played:

The Fiscal Buyer - person that writes the check

The Practical Buyer - the person that looks for all of the technicalities as to how well your product or service solves their specific challenge

The Consumer Buyer - the person, or persons, that will use your product or service.

The Coach - the person that coaches you through the sales process of the others. These can be all one person, they can be a committee of people or anything in between, but every role will be played in every sale.

Let's break each role down and also discuss why it is important to get each one's buy-in in order to make the sale.

What other solutions has the Fiscal Buyer looked at and why haven't any of them been implemented?

Not only the "What", but the "How" they buy is important, too. What buying process does the Fiscal Buyer use? How have they defined what the "right" solution looks like? Again, in these areas is where your Coach becomes an invaluable part of your selling process.

Your Coach could easily be someone at an entry level of an organization, such as a receptionist. I have made many sales based on building a relationship with receptionists and getting them to share with me information about the company, people in the company and the best way to interact with them.

Your Coach can also be a person outside of the organization you want to do business with, but has relationships, or at least a strong familiarity, with the organization. This could be a salesperson that has sold a similar product to the company, a consultant, or someone that has worked for the company in the past, to name a few.

Consumer Buyer

These are the people that will use your product or service. You have probably worked at a company where you saw a lot of buzz going on with management and then, the next thing you know, some new process, tool, software, etc. is being introduced. You look at it. You touch it. You talk to your co-workers about it. And, you all decide that it isn't right for you because it is going to make your job harder for you. It's not as easy to work with. The format of the page is different. You have an additional process to go through to do the same job. So, the project fails.

That's what I mean by getting the Consumer Buy-in or adoption. I have found that one of the best ways to get Consumer Buy-in is by offering a free trial, if possible. Once the trial is complete, then create a form to have the Consumer Buyers give you input and rate your product/service. An additional benefit to using a free trial is that, if the majority of the Consumer Buyer population favours your product/service, then you have ammunition to use with the other Buyers as to why they should go with you as their vendor-of-choice.

Practical Buyer

This is the person that makes sure your product/service meets the company's specifications. Is it the right size? Does it work with their other hardware, software? Is it user-friendly? Will it cause the company to have to make any changes, such as physically altering their facility, having additional staff training?

This person, many times more than not, is looking for a way to knock you out of the competition. They are looking for a reason to tell you no. This is only logical, because once they have eliminated all of the people they can because of what many times would be considered a minor issue, the sooner they can focus on the vendors they know meet the minimums and they can build from there.

By the way, for obvious reasons, this is a great person to have on your side and recommending you to the rest of the Buyers. It is also another reason to go into your selling situation well-prepared, either by your own research, a Coach, or both. Knowing what your Practical Buyer's minimum needs are will go a long way to setting yourself up for sales success.

Fiscal Buyer

I left this Buyer for last because he/she/they will be the one(s) that make the decision to write the check. As you have noticed, all of the Buyers up to this point had a focused agenda, their needs. Not that the Fiscal Buyer doesn't. But, especially if you're selling at the President and C-level, this person has a much broader brush stroke to be concerned about.

While the others have a more immediate view, the C-level person has the future in view. This person will be concerned, not just about the immediate cost and effects, but on-going costs and effects. They will be concerned about how your product/service will affect future plans for the company. One of the best situations you can encounter is when the perspectives of what the solution looks like, is an empty canvass. This is where you truly become a partner with the company in building the vision of what the solution looks like.

If you have the opportunity to meet with the Fiscal Buyer early on in the buying process, it is to your advantage to help that person script the vision of the solution. In this way, if you can truly be of help in solving the challenge they want you to solve, you have set the standard by which any other vendors being considered will be judged by. This puts you at a distinct advantage.

So, be a consultant, advisor, even a partner, with the Fiscal Buyer and look long-term as to how your product/service will solve the challenge(s) they are facing now and into the future.

Keep in mind that all prospects and buyers listen to the same radio station, WIIFM.

What's In It For Me. They don't care if you want to buy a new car, a house, or a boat. They want to know what you are going to do for them, both personally and for their position in the company. So, be outward focused during the selling process. As Zig Ziglar said many years ago, "If I help enough people get what they want, then, in return, I'll get what I want."

Coach

Whether you're selling B2B or B2C and you have more than one individual involved in the buying process, you will need a Coach.

Let's say, for instance, that you are selling IT software. You have found a contact at a mid-management level. For the purpose of our discussion, that person is the Practical Buyer. So, you find out what the practical and technical needs are for solving the challenge they are currently facing. Now, you need to understand how the Fiscal and Consumer Buyers see the challenge and what it will take to win them over to a sale.

Your Practical Buyer now becomes your Coach, too. Once you see that the Practical Buyer agrees that you have the solution to his/her challenge, you can ask what information they see would be valuable to the other buyers.

How would your solution help the Consumer Buyers' jobs be easier?

What would it take for them to easily adopt your software?

How has the lack of a solution so far had a fiscal impact on the company?

Step 2: Prospecting/Target Marketing and Setting Appointments

This is the life-blood of your business. There are many avenues to prospecting, web and print advertising, direct mail, telemarketing, expos, and cold-calling. What many sales people don't realize is that as you progress through each of these, the cost-per-contact becomes greater.

In most cases, salespeople are needed to consummate the sale. But, doesn't it make sense to increase the likelihood of closing sales by "softening" the prospective clients up by building name recognition and credibility by utilizing the other prospecting/marketing methods as well? Enough said about building a well-balanced marketing plan for now. Let's get into some simple rules for what most people think about when they think of prospecting.

As stated before, know who it is you need to meet with. I have worked with hundreds of sales people and many of them come from the mindset that all they need to do is set enough appointments with enough people and they will get sales. And, that's true. As the saying goes, "A blind squirrel will discover an acorn every once in a while."

It is an exhausting and discouraging way of doing business. No wonder so many salespeople don't meet their quotas and don't last long in sales. By targeting the prospecting efforts on people that have a high likelihood of wanting and being able to buy, you will have good time management and a great conversion rate.

Know the person and the company you're contacting. Do you know what is happening with the company you're about to contact? Are they being bought by another company or are they buying another company? Are their profits going up, or are they going down? Are there any significant things happening that are on their website or in the news or Internet? What about the person you're wanting to contact? Are they new to the company? Have they recently received a promotion? Is there any information about them on Facebook, Twitter or other community websites?

Have a script. Too many people think they know their product so well that they will just "wing it". They never say the same thing twice, so they never know what works, and doesn't work, when they are prospecting and setting appointments. I'm not saying to be a robot. Be conversational, but have a base of wording that you share each and every time so that you have consistency. Also, keep track anytime you make a change to your basic verbiage.

If, on Monday morning, you started using a new word, or words, in your script, document it. If you see that you are getting better results, then continue to use the new verbiage. If the results are worse than before you starting using the new verbiage, obviously you'll want to go back to using the verbiage you were before.

Again, don't change things up so often that you can't tell what works well. Give a new twist about two weeks before changing again, unless you see your results falling off fast. If that's the case, go back to "home" immediately!

Have a goal. Prospecting is usually the least glamorous and least favorite activity for salespeople. It's like running on the treadmill. If you don't set a goal for the amount of time you WILL stay on it, then you'll quit as soon as the first gasp of air comes or you start to hurt. Depending on the business and the length of the sales cycle, I recommend adding at least 5 to 10 NEW prospects each day.

So, what this means is that you're not going home, you're not leaving your desk, you're not having dinner…until you have those NEW prospects. The same applies to setting appointments. Have a goal for each day or week for the number of NEW appointments you will set. By doing this, you'll not fall into the up-and-down cycle of business and income that so many sales and business people do.

Use a good CRM system (Customer Relationship Management). With as much effort that it takes to prospect, you want to make sure that you capture the results of your work. Not just the appointments you've set, but those that aren't prospects for now, and those that will never be prospects. Duplication of your sales effort is costly. Take time to analyze the information in your CRM on a weekly basis. I like to do ratios of contacts to appointments, appointments to sales, dollars to sales, and dollars to contacts. This way you can track yourself or your salespeople on how effective you or they are being. You should see an ever increasing trend of effectiveness.

At the first sign of stagnation or reversal, you need to find out what is happening so you can immediately correct it. By the way, tracking the dollars – contacts is a great motivating tool. With that information, you know exactly how much it means to you in revenue every time a person is contacted. So, if you know you make $1000 every time you talk to a person, whether they buy or not, that keeps you and your sales team motivated to prospect!

Step 3: The presentation

When I first learned sales long ago, I was taught to control the situation. I knew the prospect needed my product, I knew more about my product that he/she did, and they just needed to sit and hear my story so I could tell them everything I knew and then ask them to sign on the dotted line.

The flow of stalls and objections would come, but I was taught how to quickly overcome each and every one of those, too. You may have sat through one of those kinds of presentations. You were interested and saw some things you wanted to know more about, so you asked a question. But, the salesperson was trained to forge forward, so he/she said something like, 'I'm on page 7 and you're on page 10. Let me catch up.' And, then they pressed through their robotic presentation. How did that make you feel?

Today's prospects are much better educated when making a buying decision than ever before. So, I have developed a way to make selling much less work. Let the customer tell me what they want and see if I can be a solution to their challenge. Not, let me see if can squeeze what I have into a box that looks like it will fit their challenge.

We have two ears and one mouth, so during the presentation, the salesperson should listen twice as much as they talk. Also, most sales trainers teach the methodologies of sales and leave out the part that really gets you the sale, the emotional investment. Remember, *people buy on emotion and support it with logic.* Unfortunately, salespeople are taught to sell on logic and then get the prospect emotionally involved. In my experience personally and in training hundreds of salespeople, the latter doesn't work.

Open with the statement:

"(Name of prospect), *you told me over the phone that you had a concern with _____, if you'll tell me more about that, we'll be able to decide if doing business together makes sense for both of us.*" Then be quiet and let the prospect talk. Take copious notes. If the prospect says something you're not sure about, stop them and say, "*Tell me more about _____*" and let them talk.

Here's a caution: Don't be too quick to share your solution. Let the Buyer elaborate on the details so that you can feedback how you will solve each detail of the challenge with your solution, but only when the time is right. Be sure to include probes that look for facts and emotions, such as:

"Tell me more about_____"
"What I hear you saying is _____"
"It sounds like you're _____"
"You seem very _____"

By using such probes, you'll direct the conversation, but let the Buyer share their "pains". It also let's them hear themselves say and feel the "pain", which is much more effective than you stating it. In fact, one of the most important tools I like to use is to find an area of "pain" and then let the Buyer live in it for a moment.

After a Buyer makes a statement like, "I'll never do something like that again", I'll say something like *"It sounds like there's a story. Do you mind sharing it with me?"*

Most of the time I get a detailed story filled with all the emotion that went along with the event. What this allows is for me to come back on the flip side and ask, *"What would it have been like if you would have had a solution? How would that have made you feel?"*

I let the Buyer bask in the warmth of the situation having gone right, instead of wrong, and I can now start to interject how my product/service could have made the latter a reality, with all of the pleasant emotions to go along with it. Now, guess what has just happened to my relationship with the Buyer. I am now associated with pleasant feelings.

Another important part of this step is using the question, *"Is there anything else I should know?"* Before moving on to any new points during this step, ask that question. The reason is that it allows the prospect to think about things one more time and they may come up with more reasons they need to buy from you.

Depending on the depth and level of the sale, this process can take anywhere from 10 minutes to an hour or more. In some cases, this will make up your entire first meeting.

Only when you have gathered all the information that you need to fully understand the prospect's needs and desires do you ask for other critical information. What impact will it have on them personally or the company if they do or don't solve the concern? What other resources are they researching to solve the concern? Why they haven't used them? Who else has to be involved in making a decision to purchase? What is their timeline for solving their challenge?

Now you can go into your video presentation, flip chart or whatever medium you're using to display your product or service. The difference is that now you are armed with what is important to them so that you can focus the presentation on what you can do for them, specifically, and leave out anything that isn't important to them.

Once done, be sure to summarize the meeting so far to make sure you and the Buyer are both on the same page. Now, here is something you must learn to do at this point. Ask the question, "Is there anything else I should know?" There may yet be something important that your prospect hasn't shared with you and you don't want to lose the sale because you didn't get that detail.

Step 4: Closing

I have seen many great presenters get to the point of closing only to see their wheels fall off. I remember one young man in particular that was wonderful at presenting, but he just wasn't bringing in the sales. So, I decided to go with him on appointments one day.

As we went to each one, they became progressively worse at the same point in each presentation, the close. He would be going along smooth and gracious and then his voice would start to crack and stutter. After the last appointment I asked him about it.

He told me that he just couldn't ask people for money. His career in sales was over.

And, so it is with so many salespeople. I have found that I can minimize or eliminate that challenge for most people. You see, most people separate the close from the rest of the presentation when, in fact, it is just a part, and a natural conclusion, to it.

When you use the steps I have discussed prior, it all flows flawlessly. Here's why: You have taken the time to understand your prospect's wants and needs, you understand why it is important to solve the concern they have, you know that they have researched other resources and haven't found a solution. Enter you on a white horse!

You have just shown your prospect that you have a solution that fits their wants and needs, you have a way of relieving the burden that was hanging over their head, you have made them feel the emotions of a bad situation and helped them feel that compared to a great situation, and you will probably make them look like a star for doing business with you. You ARE the solution! You have every right to ask for their business. In fact, if you didn't, you would be doing them a disservice. It's as simple as ending your presentation and saying, "Do you see how _____ will solve the problem of _____? Are you ready to move forward?" or "What would you like to do next?"

You may be asking, "What about stalls and objections?" With this method you should have very few, if any, to deal with. Here's how to effectively deal with stalls and objections. Don't try to do fancy footwork or give some sly answer. Your prospect is too educated. Answer it succinctly and to the point. Then, ask, "Why do you ask?" or "Why do you say that?" Probe for specifics for the question or objection and then isolate it. Let me give you an example:

Prospect/Buyer: "Your price is too high."
You: "Based on what we've discussed this can save you over time, I'm curious, why do you say that?"

Prospect/Buyer: "One of your competitors has given me a lower price."
You: "Let's explore what their price includes to make sure we're talking about the same thing. But, first, let me ask, other than the price given to you by the competitor is there anything else that would stand in our way of doing business?"

By proceeding with answering a question or objection without knowing if there are other items that stand in the way of doing business is sales hari-kari. If you've been around sales for any length of time, you made the mistake of answering a question or objection only to have one after another follow.

Especially when you're dealing with pricing, you must know if there is anything else that needs to be addressed. If you decide to discount your price and there were other things yet to deal with, it could become a win for the prospect/Buyer, but a losing situation for you.

Step 5:Follow-up

For longevity in business, you're going to need great and consistent follow-up. There are three areas where follow-up can have a huge impact on your business; prospecting, post-presentation, and no-sale.

You spend a large amount of time deciding on your target market, researching prospects within that market, and marketing to those prospects. What a waste of time to do all that work and then not follow-up! What happens many times is that a company acquires a list of "qualified" prospects of hundreds, or even thousands, of names, addresses, phone numbers, etc. and then they send direct-mail pieces and/or emails to all of them at once. I believe that this is with the hope that the stars will all align just right and a flood of responses will come in.

Think of the last time you picked up your mail at home. You look through the stack of mail for envelopes that aren't addressed to "resident" or "occupant" and then decide of what is left over what you will open. Now, keep in mind that there were probably 5-10 flyers, postcards and the like that you didn't even look at. The same is true of your business prospects. The better way is to decide on a targeted area, maybe a zip-code, an area code, some well-defined geography that is small enough to allow you to follow-up on the information you sent within ONE WEEK.

Differentiate your Business

The pieces you send should differentiate you from the pack. If it's a direct mail piece, be sure it is an odd size so that it doesn't shuffle in with the rest of the stack and get lost. An odd sized piece of mail is more likely to get handled and looked at.

If it is an email, be sure the email has something of interest in the subject line for the market you are going after. Knowing your market intimately will tell you what that is. If you're selling toys for children, a subject line might be "safe government compliant toys". Experience tells me that if you send something out to a prospect, you feel better about making the call. I have tested the theory out. I had told my group of salespeople that I had sent out a direct-mail piece to their respective territories. I showed them the piece and handed it out to each of them. Unbeknownst to them, I had only sent it out to half of their territories. But, the result was the same. Each salesperson felt more confident in making a cold-call because they thought they had been previously introduced!

So, take advantage of the confidence and energy that can be driven by marketing.

Be Strategic in your Follow-ups

You've now invested a huge amount of time and money to get your name out there, so follow-up, follow-up, follow-up.

No matter how well you qualify your prospects and appointments, no matter how well you understand your prospect's needs and wants, no matter how strong of a closer you are, there will be some sales you won't close. In today's business environment, even what used to be considered a "simple", "one-call-close" sale has turned into multiple meetings before the sale is consummated. So, here, again, follow-up is imperative.

The key in this situation is being strategic. Know what you want to accomplish at each meeting to progressively move the sale forward. Then, as you conclude each meeting, assign yourself and your prospect action steps to move to the next phase. Make absolutely sure you set a date and time for the next meeting before leaving the current one. Now here's where the follow-up comes in; as you complete your assigned tasks, call your prospect to confirm that they, too, are getting their tasks done. You must make sure that you use the information from the last meeting as to their motivation for being interested in doing business with you in front of them.

All too often business and salespeople follow-up, but don't give or remind the prospect of their motivation for taking precious time to do work on top of their day-to-day load. When that happens, the deal falls apart and the prospect doesn't do their research, or get the information, or do whatever you needed them to. The day-to-day "time-goblins" have struck again! They have probably even forgotten why they were talking to you.

Not only do you need follow-up for that, but also for the sales you close. Follow-up can be to thank a prospect or new client for the meeting or for their business. It can be to gather, or share, additional information after a meeting. It can be just to keep your name to the forefront of a prospect's mind by sharing information with them about something going on in their industry or something special you have to offer to them. A word of caution: Don't use the age-old phrase, "I was just calling to follow-up." It lacks meaning and it tells your prospect that you didn't call with a real purpose. They'll feel that you are wasting their time and won't connect you with being a partner with them in business.

Also, during your first meeting or first sale you may not have addressed all of the needs they have for products and services you provide. So, as part of follow-up, have a strategic plan on going back to your clients to discuss additional opportunities that may be present for you to help them.

A follow-up call may go something like this:

"Hi, _____! I had told you that I would keep in contact with you about the _____ that you purchased from me to make sure all is going well. So, please give me some feedback."

"That's great! I love it when my clients have a great experience with my product/service. You know, during our meeting, you said something about a need to solve a problem with _____. I think I may have just the right solution for you and I'd like to come by and meet with you see if I can be of service to you again. When could I come by and discuss that with you further? Who else would need to be at the meeting about _____? Can they meet with us, too? I look forward to seeing you then!

It takes ten times the amount of work and resources to get a new client as it does to keep a current client. So, from a time management and an income perspective, it makes sense to keep in close contact. Let me give you a personal example.

I once acquired a new client and she told me during the presentation that they were going to double their staff at that office soon, as they were closing a facility and bringing them to this one. I did my usual follow-up after the sale. After about a month, I found that there was a problem she was hesitant to tell me about until I pressed her for feedback and I was able to address it immediately. I like to be a problem-seeker so that I can be a problem-solver.

Anyway, I continued to follow-up every other month, especially during the holidays and developed a close, professional relationship. I asked her a couple of times about the move and if they had the timing set for it and she told me that it kept changing. I asked her if she might need my services again when the moved happened and she said she would give that some thought. Not long ago, I received a phone call from my client. Without an additional meeting she placed an order with me.

I made $5,000 for about 10 minutes worth of work. Great follow-up pays off.

I hope that you find this information valuable and useful and that it puts you on your way to sales success!

B2C Selling

B2B (Business to Consumer) or Retail selling, is any product or service where the customer comes to you in a store or place of business. The expectation of the salesperson is to receive this client, answer their questions and offer solutions to them, to ain their business.

Acknowledging Your Customers

If there's an important point you should take home from the world of B2C selling it's that you should always acknowledge your customer.

When I was young and working in a busy mobile phone store we often got overwhelmed with the amount of customers entering the store. The very first sales principle I was taught by my manager was that we acknowledge our customer's presence.

Personally, I think this is what makes the difference between someone that's happy to wait to be served and someone that stands there huffing and puffing and finally being quite upset when you do get around to helping them.

If you give a genuine nod of acknowledgement, say "hello, we'll be right with you", or something as simple as making eye contact and smiling then you're already off on the right foot. They instantly feel special.

It's so easy to get into the mentality of treating your customers like sheep to be herded, especially in a busy retail situation. But let me tell you, you'll be losing customers faster than anything. People like to feel appreciated and even something as simple as acknowledging that they are there can really go a long way.

Greet Your Customers Appropriately

All it takes it someone with a bad temper, someone who got up on the wrong side of the bed, or someone that's just easily put off and you could be losing sales with a bad first impression.

Greet all of your customers equally, with professionalism and respect. Try to use a friendly tone, but not too friendly and it's best if you use a neutral way to greet your clients.

"Good afternoon, how are you today?"

"Good morning, how may I help you today?"

"Hi there, I'm Josh, can I give you a hand with anything?"

One Final Point

A disturbing trend has started surfacing in America's retail scene and that's asking people questions that I think are just a little too personal. It's a fake sounding "trying to get to know you" routine. As a consumer, I hate it. It's absolutely the worst thing in the world forcing your customers to make small talk with you because you both know one thing for sure: You really don't really give a care what I had for breakfast or what I've got planned for the rest of the afternoon!

Seriously, if the talking isn't genuine and if you're not interested in what they had for breakfast, don't ask. It's as simple as that.

I'm not saying stand there in silence – just drop the facade.

Chapter 2

Selling with Good Communication

Asking Open Ended Questions

The easiest way to build rapport with your customer isn't to force casual talk and other banter, it's to get _them_ talking!

To get someone talking you need to ask the right type of question.

If you ask a question that has only a yes or no answer, then that's exactly what you'll get. Where do you go from there?

An open ended question is where you ask a pointed question that requires thought and a longer response.

The hardest people I've ever come across to chat to in a sales situation are truck drivers. They spend hours on the road not talking to anyone and 9 times out of 10 are typically known as "a man of few words". They can be a metaphorical brick wall when it comes to relating to them.

If this technique works on them (and it does) then you can use it to get almost anyone talking.

When you're about to ask a question of your customer, ask yourself first, "does this question have more than a yes or no answer?" If not, reformulate the question so it does.

Listen Carefully

Once you get that truck driver talking you'll never be able to shut him up, I can guarantee that.

Your next most important skill after crafty question creation becomes listening.

Pay attention to what they are saying, this will help you reform new questions which will lead to creating a mental check list of their needs.

I find it's often helpful to restate their needs in a casual way to let them know you understand.

This technique of confirming at every step is an instant rapport builder, it will make your customer believe that you do actually understand their issues, problems, and could possibly hold the answer they've been looking for.

It will help you get them in a positive state of mind – that of thinking "yes".

The Difference between Wants and Needs

Have you ever had a customer come up to you 100% sure that they want one thing when really they need something else?

This is because most customers don't really know exactly what it is that they need.

A need, in sales terms, is something that solves a problem or perceived problem. A want is something that is nice to have.

Personally I like to address the needs of my clients first as they more often than not highlight how the wants are not as important.

Getting to the Specifics

As you build rapport with your customer by asking them open ended questions as we discussed in the last installment, you'll begin to sort through all the requests and nut out exactly what that final check list of things your customer needs is.

It's important to continue confirming and checking on the way by restating their needs back to them in a casual manner.

ME: "So you said, your phone needs to have a camera? Why is that?"

CUSTOMER: "I'm a real estate agent and I need it to take quick photos of my properties. I'm not expecting it to be high quality."

ME: "Oh so you're a real estate agent, that's interesting, I know who to come to next time I want to buy a house! The camera in this phone should suit your needs, its 6 megapixels and takes HD photographs. So if you need a camera, do you think scheduling and calendar capabilities would be high on your list as well?"

See how this can be a natural progression of open ended questions?

Build up this list of features in your head that they need, sorting them by importance if you can. Feel free to ask them how important certain requests are if you have to. This is all information that you need to build up your internal database of requests.

How to Formulate Solutions on the Fly

When they refer to salesmanship as being a craft, what I like to think people mean is our ability to create a solution that solves people's problems all while thinking on our feet.

This isn't an easy skill to develop and I won't pretend that it is. But there are a number of things you can do to make it easier on yourself as a sales person.

Selling Value and Quality

Many salespeople make the mistake of concentrating their presentations on the fact that they are offering the best price.

This will put you in the same category as many of your competitors and devalue what you are selling.
The key to effective selling is to be the best and to be different than your competitors.

Consumers do want the best price and value for their dollar, but there's a lot to be said for positioning yourself as representing the best products with the best quality.

Craftsmanship, design and product intelligence and delivery speak loudly to everyone who is considering making a purchase.

Study Your Product

In order to take control of a sales situation and turn it around you need to have something solid backing you up.

That something solid is always going to be your product knowledge and I'm sure every sales manager around the globe just shouted "Yes, I've been trying to drill this into my sales people for decades!"

Product knowledge is something that's very personal to each sales person. Some people are quite adept at storing facts and figures in their heads, other people just need short notes to get them up to speed.

Whatever it is, you still need some in-depth familiarity with the product you're trying to sell before you can sell it with confidence.

Daily learning is required in sales as the environment changes so often. The mobile phone business for instance changes weekly. It can be quite daunting for a new sales person starting to sell phones. This is the same for any industry.

Using Your Mental Checklist

As I mentioned in the previous two steps it's important to build a mental check list of needs and wants that your customer has mentioned in talking to them.

Once you've got a mental check list that is comprehensive enough for you to form an opinion about what would be the ideal solution for your customer you can be more confident in reassuring their objections.

Pitching the Solution

When pitching the solution, make an initial suggestion and let your customer choose to hear more about why that would suit them. This is one of the most important times to be aware of your customer's body language.

Start making your way through the needs and wants of your customer addressing the most important needs first.

This is the time to state why this is the best solution for them.

Ramping Up to Ask for the Sale

In the last few steps we discussed creating a mental checklist, asking open ended questions and listening with intent so you can formulate a solution on the fly.

Now that you've pitched your solution you're at that awkward stage of asking for the sale and this is where 80% of sales people trip up.

Asking for the sale can sometimes feel a little uncomfortable, I won't disagree there. What you have to remember is that they're expecting you to ask. When you ask for the sale you're giving them permission to say "yes". If you've done your job well asking the right types of questions and keeping in mind what their true needs are then it's really a logical conclusion to the discussion.

How to Ask For the Sale

I like to approach this directly. It's like ripping off a band-aid and if you can say it with confidence in the solution that you've provided your customer will usually go with the flow because, to them, you have been giving them all the indicators that you know what you're doing.

While we previously focused on asking open ended questions, we want to do the exact opposite. You really only require a yes or no answer.

If it's a "yes", then it's time to finish the job.

What to Do About "No"?

A "No" means you've probably pitched a solution too early, meaning you're missing some information. Go back to step three and ask more open ended questions. Build your mental checklist, then ask again.

Don't be afraid of a rejection. They're still sitting there, right?

It just means they're still withholding some information, or they simply don't like what you're offering.

Knowing When to Ditch

Some sales can't be won because the customer isn't ready.

I'll let you in on a little trick that I used to do at least once a day.

If you've been through the cycle on getting all the information, building up to asking for the sale, finally "popping the question" and getting a rejection several times then you're well within your rights as a sales person to stop wasting everyone's time.

I could often be heard saying to the customer: "I don't think you're quite ready to buy something yet and I hate being all high pressure. So take these brochures, think on it for a few days and give me a call if you've got any questions."

I'd say more than half of them would be ready to buy within the week.

The Green Light

Now that you've gotten to "Yes", you need to lock that sale in as quickly as possible. It's kind of like the last 100 yards in a marathon run and you should be sprinting.

Once you've received a green light from your customer your whole purpose now should be about getting the paper work done efficiently, confirming the order details and getting any further credit or administrative information to the client.

The process of closing the deal needs to be easy to conduct – make sure your business processes reflect that. There's nothing worse than having a willing customer and having so many delays that they lose confidence and reconsider.

Reassure your customer, thank them for their business and tell them they've made the right choice. There's not much more to this stage really.

Selling to Customers You Know is Easier than Selling to Strangers

There's an old adage in sales that selling your products and services to existing customers is easier than selling them to new customers.

I totally agree with that sentiment, you can and will always have better ratios with existing customers when it comes to comparing cost of acquiring new customers and gross profit. You simply don't have to market or sell as hard with existing clients.

I like to take this one step further though and start the up-selling process early.

When you're busy closing the deal, it's simple to ask them if there are any other things you can help them with. I like to discuss their current arrangement for products or services that I know I can offer alternatives for. In this way, I can offer an incentive to switch, upgrade or purchase something they wouldn't normally have considered – it's an opportunity to create a deal that is too sweet to resist.

Using this technique in my sales career I maintained a higher gross profit average per hour than any other sales person. Simply put, I was the best person at linking a sale through our whole business and thus my GP/hour was higher.

I've spoken to sales people that use this technique all the time and swear by it as well. One person uses training sessions with existing clients (and even groups of existing clients) to showcase new products and services his company offers but may not be sold to customers initially. This way he gets the benefit of having their full attention in the training session they are conducting as well as having a captive audience for showing off some of the other products on sale and relating them back to their client's needs.

Up-selling: Timing is Everything

There is one key to making this up selling technique work. In order to link your whole business through the one sale you need to get your timing right and deliver the pitch more casually than your original sale.

I call it the "while I'm here" effect.

The while I'm here effect basically means they are in a more willing and accepting mood than prior to accepting your offer. Once they're sitting down and we're busy closing the sale, that's the opportune time to ask for an up-sell.

Think about what other services or products your business offers for sale. Ask your clients if they have these things taken care of. If they do, ask them if they're happy with their current provider and mention a potential deal you could make if they were to buy some more items from you.

Because you already have the first sale locked in you should be able to afford (literally) to be more flexible with the pricing on your later offers. Make it enticing, after all the cost of acquiring their business for this new sale is essentially $0.

Learn From the Masters – Self Referrals in Action

Think this technique of linking sales across your whole business is new? Think again. Amazon and other online companies have been using this technique to build their business online and other offline companies have been using this technique for even longer.

Think carefully about how you can build your offer as you're closing your sale. By encouraging your customer to buy more while you are there, you can boost your gross profit margins incredibly. It seriously adds up.

Chapter 3

7 Steps to Successful Selling

The Seven Steps to Successful Selling are the basis of all sales calls and you should make this a priority to thoroughly learn them.

Copy the following Seven Steps for Successful Sales and keep it handy to prepare and reflect before each customer conversation.

Make some notes for personal reference that pertain to your specific product or service for each of the seven steps. Put it in your own words. Know your process and listen intensely to your customers. Know where your customers are within the seven step process. Take care of your customers and continue your conversations after every sale to repeat the cycle and nurture your pipeline.

Seven Steps to Successful Sales

- Introduce Yourself, then Shut-Up and Listen
- Why the Offer is Important to the Customer
- Get Confirmation, then Explain the Details

- Credibility, Show the Customer Why You can be Trusted
- What to do and What it will Cost
- Schedule Next Steps
- Ask for the Sale

1. Introduce Yourself, Then Shut-Up and Listen

The sales experience is not about the salesperson, it is about the customer. It is a courtship ritual to determine if the customer values the goods or services enough to invest in them by making a purchase. There is only one way to find out what the customer values, wants or needs and that is to listen intensely. If you are thinking about the next thing that you are going to promote then you can not concentrate on what the customer is telling you. Rather, think about how you can repeat what the customer is saying in your own words and you will be forced to listen intently to what they tell you.

A successful salesperson can reflect the emotion as well as the content of a customer conversation.

2. Why the Offer is Important to the Individual Customer

As new sales representatives learn about the company, products or services that they represent, it is natural to initiate conversations by spewing facts and features like a walking commercial. Don't assume that the customer cares how you do something, how long you have done it or what you have been told makes you unique. The customer has a life with priorities, deadlines and responsibilities of his or her own. Show the customer what aspects of your offer are important from the customer perspective and resist the urge to talk about any other things that are not relevant. Of course, you will only know this if you have listened to your customer.

A successful salesperson focuses only on the specific attributes of the offer that are relevant to the customer.

3. Get Confirmation then Explain the Details

Get buy-in from the customer that you are on the right track. Ask the customer for feedback to confirm that the focus is on the appropriate facts, features or figures. Once you have provided feedback on your value as it pertains to the initial customer requirement, it is common for some customers to change the focus. This is an opportunity to find out if the customer has additional concerns or considerations. Listen with intensity and restate customer focus and topics in short sentences, reiterating each item that is important to the customer.

Then explain the details of your offer that support all of these interests.

A successful salesperson keeps the customer involved during the process of explaining relevant details of the specific offer.

4. Credibility, Show the Customer Why You can be Trusted

If the offer is on target with the customer requirements then it is appropriate to demonstrate reasons that the customer should trust you. This may be accomplished by using specifications for products, white papers and case studies for services, independent articles or references. The manner of demonstrating credibility varies significantly by industry and market. If there are no documents or history to use as reference, it is possible to demonstrate credibility by making promises and keeping them. A promise may be as simple as a commitment to follow-up with additional information by a specific time. Even if the customer was a referral and credibility was implied, never take it for granted.

A successful salesperson earns the trust of every single customer through commitments and actions.

5. What to Do and What it will Cost

In addition to providing the price, also provide the details of what needs to be done to complete the transaction and what will happen after the sale. If the customer needs to take some action before, during or after the purchase then be sure to explain this in detail. In some cases there may be a registration, license or contract associated with the sale, so be sure to remove any mystery or doubt by stating the facts. Make sure that the customer is aware of any additional requirements or renewals. As an example, it would be incredibly disappointing for a customer to excitedly unpack a new printer and then discover that is it necessary to go back to the store for cables to connect it to a computer. Keep the customer satisfied and confident by providing step-by-step explanations and expectations.

A successful salesperson knows the process and educates the customer.

6. Schedule Next Steps

In many cases there may be several steps in the sales cycle. If ongoing negotiation is necessary then schedule the next meetings and milestones. If registration or installation is necessary after the sale then initiate discussions to accommodate the customer schedule. For significant purchases and investments it may be necessary for the customer to review budget or finances, in which case it is appropriate to schedule periodic follow-up to accommodate these considerations.

A successful salesperson fills the pipeline by keeping a consistent schedule for continuous customer conversations.

7. Ask for the Sale

Don't assume that the customer is going to ask for the sale. Ask for the sale to determine if it is time to stop selling and time to start processing the purchase and assisting with the appropriate next steps to support the customer. Some sales associates are so passionate about the product that they keep promoting it long after the customer has made a decision to purchase and can actually lose a customer in the process. Stop pouring when the glass is full.

A successful salesperson will periodically pause to ask for the sale.

Chapter 4

Tools of the Trade

One of the exciting elements of the sales business is the fact that it only requires a few items of proficiency in order to be successful. These items are all easy to articulate and well within your grasp. They are:

Knowledge and skill

A strategic attitude

Credibility

Attainable goals

Product professionalism

You will notice that all of these elements are connected in nature.

You need only to excel in these areas to enjoy on-going success in sales, however, should you ignore any one of these items then it will negatively impact your overall sales results.

Champion sales achievers are all extremely proactive in their efforts to maintain these few disciplines.

Your knowledge and skill set with respect to the industry you are in and your sales ability are completely in your control.
Regardless of your current sales ability and background, you should be devouring all of the training made available to you.

One thing that all high sales achievers possess is that they are well schooled and have a thirst for new ideas. Knowledge is not only power - but a prerequisite for success.

In order for you to become a leader in relationship sales, you must make a conscious decision to:
a) know the product/service thoroughly and
b) refine your selling and communication skills.

If there are any areas of the product/service that you are not clear on, then do whatever it takes to immediately become an expert.
Make a commitment to not only read the material, but also to practise it and role play with your colleagues.

Important Notice

Once you have begun the process of refining your knowledge and skill set, you will project a tremendous level of confidence and expertise into your sales calls.
People will respond favourably to your

recommendations as you will be well educated and capable of offering consultative solutions.
There is no question that our attitudes have a dramatic impact on our level of success.

In professional selling, we need to be pro-active on a daily basis in possessing a "strategic attitude".

This simply means that we must use our attitude, our emotional state, to our advantage.

Outstanding salespeople understand that their perspective on products, price, the market price, profitability and opportunity is always self-fulfilling.

Your strategic attitude should have:

- passion for representing your products and services ;
- commitment to the ongoing refinement of knowledge and skill
- appreciation of your resources and utilize them fully.

Remember that you now hold a fantastic opportunity to provide exceptional product-driven solutions to society. A critical aspect to your success will be able to maintain and relive your enthusiasm on an ongoing basis.

In order to gauge whether your attitude is an

asset or a detriment to your business, take the time to honesty and thoroughly answer the following questions:

- How do I feel about the quality of the products and services offered?
- What is it about the portfolio that mostly benefits people?
- Why would someone want to purchase our products/services?
- How do you really feel about selling products and services designed to help families and small businesses better manage their finances?

Chapter 5

ABC's of Successful Selling

A = ATTRACTION

A is for attraction marketing. Selling is so much easier if you can figure out how to become a magnet for hot prospects. Attraction marketing devices are what I recommend. A seminar, a free report, a special bonus will attract prospects. Focus on them, not on you.

B = BELIEVE

To make it in selling, you must have belief in yourself. You need a belief in your ultimate success. You need to believe that you will make it despite how tough things have been for you in the past. Be strong and believe that you will win. You will!

C = CONSTANT CONTACT

C is for constant contact which is what you will need to be doing to keep your customers coming back to you. Make a plan to call all your past clients soon. Call just to say "hi" and build the relationship if you want referrals, stay in touch.

D = DELIVER

If you don't deliver what you promise, you won't last very long in sales. Under promise and over deliver should be your motto. Give them more than what they pay for.

E = ENTHUSIASM

Without it, you lose. With it, you win. Start your day with positive mental gymnastics to stay fit mentally. The trick? Be enthusiastic, act enthusiastic. Play some loud, upbeat music, listen to a positive podcast. Put a little bounce in your step. Get excited about life.

F = FOLLOW-UP

F is for follow-up and follow-through. Selling is a relationship. It's like a marriage. The wedding is only the beginning. The goal is the long-term. The same thing applies to selling. Keep servicing your clients. What one thing have you put off following up on? Do it now!

G = GOALS

Goals are vital to success and mental health.
Go to a psychiatric hospital and see if any of
the patients have clearly defined, time-dated,
exciting, written goals. You and I both know
they wouldn't have any goals. Now, go find
the top income-earner in your industry and
ask if they have goals. I think you know what
response you would get. Are your goals set?

H = HARD WORK

Want lots of money without hard work? Buy
a lottery ticket! Selling can be difficult. It can
take you away from your family. We've all
missed our share of meals with the family.
You must be willing to do whatever it takes
to win - within reason, of course.

I = INTENSITY

Intensity is the willingness to get serious
about what it is you are selling. It's a
willingness to go the extra mile, stay a little
longer, try a little harder, work a little
smarter. It's doing massive activity to ensure
your sales success. If it's worth playing this
selling game, it's worth playing with
intensity.

J = JUST DO IT

Forget all the excuses. Don't wait until all the lights are green before you go after your goal. Don't wait until the delivery system is perfect, or until the merger, the new boss or next month. Just do it!

K = KEEP LEARNING

Sell, sell, sell and all will be well. How? Learn, learn, and you'll earn, earn, earn.

L = LISTEN

L is for listening, one of the most needed skills a salesperson could acquire. If you are talking more than the prospect, you lose. Stop talking and start listening. Once you understand what they need, you can offer your solution. It will be difficult to do this, if you haven't shut up enough to listen. You have two ears and one mouth – listen twice as much as you talk!

M = MANIPULATION

Manipulation is about deceit, control and personal gain. Selling is about relationship, trust, integrity, the opposite of manipulation. Steer clear of training that tries to teach how to "influence" and "power techniques to get the prospect to buy". People buy because they trust you. Manipulation techniques, even though some work, will only cost you money in the long run.

N = NO

The sale begins when the prospect says "No". It's not a bad word, it only means "no" to the picture they have in their head about what you are selling. It means that you have not sold them the picture in your head; the benefits of buying what you are selling. Paint some more.

O = OBJECTIONS

O is for objections. You need to start thinking of objections as your friend. They tell you that the prospect is interested. If I have no interest in something, I wouldn't be objecting to anything. I'm not interested. So, at the next objection you hear, rejoice ... they're still interested.

P = PAYCHECK

Remember that your paycheck is determined not by your company or your boss but by what you think. If you want a bigger paycheck, start thinking bigger thoughts. Money is the reward for service rendered. Render more service and you'll receive greater reward.

Q = QUESTIONS

Q is for questions. Questions are your best ally in selling. Ask questions, double the amount of questions you ask. Don't start talking about your product or service until you have asked the client about their needs, wants, goals, ability to pay, authority to buy. Ask, Ask, Ask.

R = RELATIONSHIP

Selling is about relationships. If you want to last and make money, treat your customers like you would a spouse. Selling is like a marriage. Look at everything you do in sales from the marriage relationship context. Will this lead to a divorce or help the relationship. Everyone hates divorce.

S = SALES

S is for sales, an honourable profession. Feel proud that you do what you do. If every one of us salespeople stopped doing what we do for just one day, we'd cripple the world economy. You really matter!

T = TRUST

The whole role of a salesperson is to deepen the level of trust that your prospects have about you. Let's face it, selling is a process of turning over something you love (money) to a person you barely know (salesperson) for a product you hope will do what he/she says. They have a justifiable reason to fear. Trust lowers fear. Don't do anything to jeopardise the trust factor.

U = U-TURN

U-turns in cars is when you make a complete turn from the direction you are going. Salespeople need to do this often too. Mental U-turns. If you have been negative this past week, then make a U-turn in your attitude. Make a U-turn when it comes to self-pity, blaming others, or limiting thinking.

V = VICTORY

V is for victory. Victory is ensured if you have the right thoughts, fuelled by the right emotions which will move you into the right action to produce the right result. For example, the right thought might be a higher income, one that is fuelled by the right emotion, like excitement and pride, which will move you into the right action which is making more calls.

W = WINNERS CIRCLE

W stands for winners circle. A winners circle is a small group of people who will ultimately give you referrals. Every salesperson needs a winners circle. Find 10, 20 or 30 influential people who have access to your target market and service them to death. Communicate what you are doing every few weeks. Drop them notes, call them, do things for them.

X = XYLOPHONE

Okay, I struggle with X. Give me a break!

Y = YOU

You are responsible for the results of your life. You alone can make the changes necessary to alter those results. You alone can put into action a plan to make your life better, your sales higher and your happiness fuller. The beauty is that it's easy once you take responsibility for "You".

Z = ZEST

Zest for life, zest for people, zest for winning. You already have it because you are who you are. You are a salesperson and I'm thrilled to be in the same profession as you.

Chapter 6

Make a Fortune in Sales

I happen to know some very intelligent people. I happen to know some very creative people. I even know some people whom I would consider brilliant. And, I know some people who have made a fortune in sales.

The funny thing is that some of the brilliant people are broke and some of the rich salespeople are not particularly bright, some are even rather dumb.

Do you have to be intelligent to make it in sales? Not really, I'm pretty good proof of that fact! So, what does it take to make a lot of money in sales?

Well, as I see it, you need two things - an ability to dream and a good selling strategy. Both are important, just think about it for a moment.

I know some pretty smart people with big dreams but they don't make a lot of money. I know a lot of pretty good salespeople who don't make much money because they haven't learned the skill of creative dreaming and held that mental picture long for them to see it materialize.

Dreaming should not be confused with goals, goal setting or goal-achieving. Dreaming is holding a mental picture of an ambition or an idea. There is nothing wrong with dreaming. We were often punished as children for dreaming. So, many of us have stopped doing it. We don't do it enough because we have to be "realistic". Remember every good idea started out as a dream.

Often we teach and train on how to set and achieve goals. But we need to realise that there is a level about goals that is a great motivator and that level is called dreams.

So, maybe it's time for us to stop for a while and dream some good dreams. How would you spend your days if you had exactly the life you wanted? Who would you spend time with and where would you go? What would it be like there? How would you feel? Let yourself go with your dreams.

Surf the dream level. For a moment forget about obstacle, plans, money or anything else that "realistic" people will remind you about far too often!

Fear keeps people from dreaming

Fear of rejection is the second biggest fear we all have in common. Salespeople know this far too well. So what do you do to overcome the fear? First, like any fear, you confront it head on.

People fear speaking in front of others more than almost anything. That's why I recommend that people join Toastmasters. It's an international organization that helps people have confidence in public speaking. I once told a friend that I felt he was at exactly the right place emotionally because he was afraid of the goal he had just set. A good measurement for growth is fear. Fear is not something to avoid. Not confronting the fear of rejection in selling is a costly choice.

Make a list of the things you fear the most and set a plan in motion to conquer them. Deal with them straight on. Don't retreat, move forward. This positive feedback will allow you to move forward in the dream process.

It doesn't cost anything to dream. So, why not dream often and in grandiose terms? Most of the highest paid salespeople dream lofty dreams.

No more effort is required to aim high and dream big dreams. So, get your mind focused on great dreams even if it seems ridiculous.

Even if it seems "impossible" today, you are just an idea away from total and fabulous success.

The skill that is needed is what I call dream focus. You can have your heart's desire and earn a lot in selling but you've got to stop looking at today's bank balance, your current problems or sales sheets. Stay focused on where you want to go and you will get there.

The second ingredient is a successful selling strategy.

A wise professor once said, "Ambition without application only leads to frustration."

You can be dream-focused but if you have a bad selling strategy then I think you will be very frustrated.

No flow

If, you are going to make a lot of money in sales, you will need to develop a system of constantly attracting a flow of good, solid, qualified leads. The proper selling strategy says that you must commit to a system of lead generation regardless of how busy you've become.

Many sales people have a "prospect a little, sell a little, prospect a little, sell a little" routine going on. We train salespeople to "prospect a lot, prospect some more, prospect even further, now sell, sell, sell." "Bite off more than you can chew, then chew like crazy!"

Find out how many prospects you need to get one sale then do whatever you have to do, to consistently attract that amount of prospects to you.

For example, if you need 23 prospects to make a sale, then you better block every Wednesday and Thursday morning for email or phone prospecting and stick to that regardless.

You might decide that you need to send out 50 emails every week to get the number of appointments to close the amount of business you need. Do that, no matter what! Keep the flow going!

One-on-one selling

I would much rather sell to 400 or 500 people at a time then one at a time. Makes sense don't you think? Then why are so many salespeople still selling one-on-one? Why don't you put together at an Attraction Marketing Event (AME) and have 100 prospects come to you, identify that they are predisposed to buy what you are selling and make a presentation to them all at the same time.

An AME is like a seminar, a trade show or a conference. This will work for many of you. I have worked with numerous sales professionals who have used AME's to sell everything from automobile repairs to beauty salon equipment.

Shaking trees selling

The approach most people take to selling (which will pretty much guarantee failure) is the "shaking tree" method of selling. They are told that selling is a numbers game and that if they shake enough trees, some fruits will fall. The problem is that it takes time and energy to shake trees. Sure, selling is a numbers game and the more you shake, the more fruit will fall.

I think it's smarter to make the fruit come to you. This is easily done by selling with Attraction Marketing Devices (AMD). An offer of a free special report or a free webinar is a good example of an AMD. They are inexpensive and if you done correctly will make the prospect come directly to you.

Little actions produce little results

If, you want to win big in selling, then get moving. You can do a lot more than you are doing now. You can do it faster and you can do it smarter. Think bigger and demand more from yourself and those you work with.

So, make a decision to increase the amount presentations you make. You can make more calls! You can see more people. You can sell more. You can.

Poor presentation

As a salesperson, you must look good, sharp and clean. You are a reflection of not only the product or service you sell but the company that employs you.

If you are going to err, err on the side of crispness and sharpness. Then the verbal presentation needs to be just as alive and enthusiastic. Never tire, never weaken and never get bored with your message.

Now not forever

Selling isn't about closing the deal. It's about developing a long-term relationship. Selling isn't like a date or a one-night stand. It's more like a marriage.

You'll starve in selling if you are focused on now instead of forever.

If you only contact your customers when you want something from them, like a referral or another order, you are focused on now. If you get a referral from them and never call to say thank you, you are focused on now.

If you remember your client's birthdays and send a card with a nice note, you are focused on forever. If you have someone who gives you referrals, you keep them updated as to the status of the referral and buy them a nice bouquet of flowers after the referral buys, you are focused the forever.

One-off selling

If, you are selling a person only once, you will not make much money in selling. It's so hard to keep finding the one-only sales.

Instead, you should concentrate on building a "Winner's Circle of Influence" which consists of people who can refer others to you. By keeping in contact with past clients, (and that doesn't means calling them every two weeks looking for referrals), you can have them repurchase and tell their friend about you.

It's called word-of-mouth selling. It someone buys what you are selling, you can bet your last dollar that he or she will have friends or colleagues who will buy the same thing.

Chapter 7

Learn to Hang in There

Selling can be tough on a person. It can be tough on a family. Many people lack the mentality to hang in there through the tough times. You can control your thoughts. You can practice perspective by changing the way you interpret your circumstances, situation, and environments.

The task is not to see a new world but to see the world with new eyes. The people who can change the way they view their worlds will win without fail.

A stranger chanced upon several workers in a small town in Italy. Curious and interested, he began to inquire from the workers as to what they were doing.

"I'm laying bricks," said the first worker. After a few minutes of idle chat, he asked another worker, "What are you doing?" he continued, "Laying bricks, eh?" The other worker somewhat indignantly responded, with shoulders straight and firmness of voice, "Laying bricks? No sir, I am building a cathedral." Both workers were working on the same job. One saw his task as laying brick upon brick upon brick, while the other saw a work being offered to the glory of God. Two people, two perspectives.

Why is it that some salespeople choose to see the worst in a situation while the others choose to see the best in the same situation? Why do some people constantly see what's gone wrong while the others look for what's right? Which one do you think will succeed further on this great journey we're on?

Everyone has obstacles. Everyone needs perspective in the face of those challenges. Your response to dealing with the storm of life will delicate the results you achieve.

What follows, are practical solutions to dealing with those times in life when everything seems to be going the opposite to your preferences.

Hang in there and Learn

The challenge of life will come.

The only place on earth that we know of where there are no problems is the cemetery. Everywhere else will be hit by the storms of life. If you remember that there is something to learn in every problem, then you can learn to grow by the storms rather than being crushed by them.

Take a good look at the obstacles in your path and instead of cursing them and wishing them away, ask yourself what you can learn from your situation. How can you become a better person through them? Remember, above every stormy cloud is a bright sun which never fades. There is something to learn in every adversity!

Hang in there and Find the Gem

There are two sides to every coin. The Chinese call this the Yin/Yang principal. Every negative has a positive opposite. You just have to look for it. One person's disaster will become the vehicle for another person to become wealthy. See your challenges in life as blessings in disguise and try to uncover the hidden opportunities.

During the great depression, not everyone went belly-up. Some people actually became rich. When you see a problem, you also need to see an opportunity. One of the fastest ways to become wealthy is to solve someone's problems or difficulties.

Many successful businesses today have been born of someone's problem. Take the man who took surplus sawdust from the lumber mills free of charge and formulated several wood-burning products from it. He saw the lumber yards had a problem with excess sawdust. Other people didn't know what to do with it – he acted and began a wonderful business.

Hang in there and be Patient

Every problem will go away. Either it will change or you will. No problem is permanent. It can't be permanent because everything is in a constant state of flux; everything changes. Look at your problem and ask, "Will this matter in five years from now? What about next year?"

Worry is useless. Instead of being ready to give in, just remember that every problem has a limited lifespan. Things will get better. Seek to grow. Tough times never last, but tough people do.

Worry is like a rocking chair; it will give you something to do, but it won't get you anywhere.

Hang in there and Think

There are no problems, there's only a shortage of ideas. Problems are not problems, ideas are the problems. Every single problem, challenge, or storm you face today has as its solution, an idea waiting to be used.

If you could only understand that the only thing standing between your current problem, and the wiping away of it, is nothing but an idea.

So, get your eyes off your problems and onto the solution. You may not be able to do anything about what has happened, but you surely can and should do something about finding a solution.
The solution may seem like a fantasy right now, but keep in mind that the airplane was nothing but a fantasy until two brothers started searching for ideas to solve their fantasy. Fantasies can become reality.

Hang in there and be Grateful

Everyone has problems. The man with holes in his shoes is upset until he met the man with no feet. You're not alone. Everyone has storms to face. The people who are winning the most in life often have the biggest challenge in front of them.

The people who win the most in life are often the biggest risk takers.
Since you're not alone, why not align yourself with others who may be facing what you are facing. You should perhaps solve your problems together.

Never forget that the greater the obstacle, the greater the opportunity.

Chapter 8

Get More Clients by Giving Talks

Any seminar, webinar, workshop, speech, talk, panel is a great opportunity to:

- attract prospects to you in a cost-efficient manner
- build a solid, profit-making database in a hurry
- make a sales presentation to hundreds at a time, instead of one on one.
- get publicity that sells your product and services to people who can't attend and to enhance your professional image,
- get people in the audience to become paying clients?

How to Fill the Room

- Hold it at a strategic location. Parking and proximity are important.
- Place on-line ads in industry newsletters and local papers. Usually,

3 or 4 days before the event for a Free Seminar, longer for paid seminars.

- Email invitations or sales letters.
- Send out brochures.
- Print tickets with a price on it then give them away complimentary.

The 3 PROFIT Zones

PROFIT Zone A: Making Money Prior to the event

The main idea is that seminars, talks, speeches can be profitable and effective ways of attracting people to you. The ultimate goal is to get business in the door. Remember the first rule for growing any business is*: "How Can I Attract More People?"*

1. People love the word FREE. But a seminar is no bargain, even if it's free, unless people know what benefit they are going to get from it;
2. Always sell what people will get by attending. Speak directly to the prospect.
3. Advertise the event well.
4. Create an incentive or offer to get them to act NOW.
5. Focus on the client and what they want. What do you think - does the client care about the seminar, even if

it's free, or do they care about getting the benefit you say you can offer?

PROFIT Zone B: Making Money at the event

To begin with, you can't get business from people until you know two things: what's bothering them and/or what objective they want to achieve.
How do you get this crucial information? Easy - Ask for it and LISTEN.

Before you say one word...

Have them fill in a survey. This allows you to collect information about your prospects for several reasons:

- You can find out about their buying habits.
- You can collect information that might be valuable to others and sell it to them.
- You can market that information to sponsors and non-competing businesses.
- You can figure out what their problems, concerns, interests and fears are then fill those needs.

What we do is have everyone fill in a one page survey. They all do it! If they don't they don't get in. We are giving them a solid two hour seminar for free, I don't think giving them two minutes to fill out a questionnaire is unreasonable.

Getting information from your prospects is more important than giving information to your prospects If you're going to be a success using workshops to get clients, you need to learn right away that the information you *get* from clients is infinitely more valuable than the information you *give* to clients. In other words, finding out from a prospect via survey or questionnaire, that they have a want you can satisfy, enables you to control the sales process. *Giving* information on what you can do for them, puts the prospect in control of the sales process – Exactly where you don't want them to be.

That doesn't mean that you should skimp on content. Whatever is said should be of immediate and tangible benefit to those attending the seminar, webinar or workshop. The main part of the event should be free from commercials. If you give solid solutions for one hour, it is perfectly acceptable to take 10 to 20 minutes at the end to sell your product or service.

How to Make the Seminar Worthwhile

Put on a first class event.

So many people have told me that they like the idea of selling at seminars but they can't

give a speech if their life depended on it.
Then hire someone who can.

Provide handouts.
You should have some very client-centered
handouts for your event.

Give a special offer.
Package what you sell in such a way that
people will buy it because they are at the
event.

Get others to pay for everything.
If you do things right, you can have others
pick up the entire costs associated with your
seminar or workshop.

*PROFIT Zone C: Making Money After The
Event*

Here are a few things you can do to cash in
after the seminar:

Send emails the next day. Give them another
chance to buy. Give them another offer but
contact them immediately.

Next, follow-up with a telephone call and
attempt to get an appointment.

You could consider sending them an email
informing them about additional
information or products.

Re-contact them frequently, once a month for the next few months. People's lives change. They might not immediately need what you were selling at the seminar but a lot can change in 4 months. Stay in touch.

Chapter 9

The 5 Most Expensive Words

- Can't

- Blame

- Passive

- Conformity

- Quit

There are certain words which should be deleted from the vocabulary of each salesperson. These words should never be uttered by the person who wishes to succeed in the profession of selling. Every time a salesperson says these words, every time a manager uses them to characterize a salesperson it costs somebody, somewhere, a lot of money.

Using any of these five words, or practised in anyway in one's behaviour is the surest way to sales mediocrity at best, sales poverty at worst.

Can't

Sales Manager: "I want you to increase your sales by at least
26% over the next 12 months. What's your response?" Salesperson: "It 'can't' be done!"

If you honestly believe that your current sales results are the best you can expect, then, you are probably right. Why is it though, that a relatively newcomer can occupy a desk right next to yours, sell exactly the same product or service as you and break all the office sales records? Why do some people earn $50,000 in sales commissions and someone just a few desks away earns $250,000? Much of it has to do with whether or not they accept the weak-minded philosophy of "Can't."

Success comes in CAN

Why not look at challenging situations with the view to solving the problem rather than being swamped by it. When I face challenges in selling, and I face some huge problems, I never permit my mind to accept the "Can't" option. There is ALWAYS a solution. I'm always only one idea away from solving whatever obstacle is in my path.

I might not know "how," but I believe that something can be done. My job is to believe that solutions come to those who refuse to be the victim of circumstances.

Blame

First of all, understand that nobody can make you mad. You do that all by yourself. If you choose to get involved in blaming, you might as well go get a salaried job somewhere. There is no way to succeed in selling if you are constantly pointing your fingers at others as the cause of what is going on in your life.

Understand that if you are to win, you must accept responsibility for your life. The sales you make, the attitude you have, the emotional state you find yourself in, is due to some choices you have made.

Your sales results have little to do with how your company is managed. Your sales sheets are not low because the economy or the government or your family, it has to do with you and with you only.

Are you using some strategies which are ineffective? Perhaps, but whose responsibility is that? Who needs to discover new and more effective methods of selling?

This word is like a disease in your mind.

Take responsibility for your life. Never point the finger at someone else. If you do remember that 3 other fingers are pointing straight back at you.

Passive

I have been working with salespeople for the past 30 years. I've heard and seen enough of them to know, without a doubt, that they leave so much of their business to chance and luck. I call it the "Hope & Pray" technique of sales success.

They hope and pray for sales but wait passively for their phones to ring. They hope and pray for referrals but do nothing to get them. They hope and pray people that they will earn more than they did last year but they don't improve their selling skills. They hope and pray that the manager will get off their back but they refuse to move into action, hoping instead things will get better all on their own.

I've never seen the phone ring all by itself. There are no significant increases in income without salespeople deciding what they want changed, developing a plan to change it, moving into action and being held accountable for the success.

What I so often see, is salespeople accepting the norm and not actively pursuing the keys to sales success. Let's take referrals for example. Most salespeople wait passively for referrals to come in. They rarely do, so they forget about the notion. Can you remember how much easier it is to sell through referrals? Wasn't the sale almost in the bag within the first few minutes because you were in there, thanks to a referral? Isn't that one of the surest ways to sales success? It sure is.

Why do retail establishments wait passively for customers to come to their store? Why wouldn't they create effective marketing campaigns to attract people? Why wouldn't they do a cross-marketing campaign with the next door shop and sell each other's services? Why wouldn't they create some compelling reason for people to move into action? If they offered some special deal, put a deadline on it and created some life around their establishment wouldn't they be better off than sitting in their store waiting for business to come to them?

Conformity

The problem for so many companies is a reluctance to try different things.

Most methods of prospecting were developed in the 1960's and little has changed since then for most people. We have been told that prospecting is a function of rejection. If you knock on enough doors you will make a certain amount of sales. I challenge this approach. I am one of the most positive people you will ever meet but even I could not withstand rejection type selling. Most of the books, articles, and training, teach people to simply not take it personally. Not take it personally? How do you do that?

No, instead I'm advocating breaking away from the way everyone else does it and sell without rejection. I'm all for creating systems to attract more leads than you know what to do with. How different would your attitude and motivation be if you went to work tomorrow morning knowing that you had 300 qualified leads from people who were ready to buy what you sell?

So much of selling today is based on the dangerous word "conformity." People follow the crowd. I call it the herd mentality. If the masses are doing something, I recommend doing the exact opposite. If nobody in your industry has a marketing package, you be the first. The masses are traditionally wrong, especially about the earning of money.

What the selling world needs are success-minded individuals who are willing to challenge the status-quo. "If you always do what you have always done, you will always get what you have always got."

Quit

So many people believe that they will sell more if they were only working for another company, selling some other product, working in a different market but there is only one problem with that: You take YOU with you wherever you go.

You never know when you are just around the corner from winning in a big way. So the next time you think about packing it in and making a move think about staying put and working through your current problems. The grass is not greener on the other side. If a light came on in your car which indicated there were problems with your engine, you wouldn't take a hammer and smash the light. Sure the light would go "off" but that would not do anything to relieve the problem with the engine. The same applies to salespeople. The real problem is your poor performance. Taking a hammer to the red light (your company, your boss) will not solve your basic problem. Solve that and you will enjoy a life of prosperity in selling.

Chapter 10

Prospecting Strategies

The most valuable commodity any salesperson possesses is "time." It is self-evident that while everyone is blessed with 24 hours each day, many salespeople do much more with their time than others.

Critical to making the most of one's time is ensuring that people who consume your time are likely to do business with you. Of course, to increase the possibility of this happening requires more than effort on your part. Some people simply could not do business with you even if they wanted to. When you spend time with these people you are wasting valuable selling time and reducing your opportunities for success. You are spending time on non-money-making activities. Not something you want to spend a great deal of time doing.

Understand the importance of qualifying

You may have a potential client value your opinion because they feel you have some philosophical or business compatibility, but it is a long way to confirm a sale to that client.

For this reason, it is appropriate to build places into your sales interviews to gather the information that you will need if you are to sell with confidence. There is no single moment when it is best to find out certain characteristics about a prospect. This process is ongoing.

However, it is wise to get considerable information early in your encounter. You may discover that a prospect simple does not hold sufficient potential to warrant a major investment of time, effort and even expense.

When "qualifying" your prospect there is always the possibility of appearing too inquisitive. It is important that your prospect feels at ease; that rapport is not damaged. Before you begin any part of your sales effort that will focus in gathering information from your prospect, I recommend some very specific terms of reference.

Use the proven introduction method

"(Prospect's name), if we are to be of service to you, it's important that I get the answers to a few questions. Do you mind if I ask you these questions?"

Notice two words that are especially important in this phrase. First, the word "we" is relevant. The word "we" implies that you represent more than just yourself and that asking these questions is part of your normal duties and practise. It is standard procedure. It creates the impression that there is a group of people standing behind the product/service you are offering. Second, the word "these" is vital. It implies that you intend to ask some very specific questions, questions with a purpose; a planned series of questions.

This reference avoids any inference that you are about to begin a barrage of pointless questions. Qualifying can be a sensitive time during any sales interaction. You must avoid any appearance of prying or meddling. A preface to your questions will reduce the possibility of your prospect resenting your questions.

Determine the five insight areas

When a prospect gives you a go-ahead, you have the opportunity to gain important insights into:

- Needs
- Wants
- Authority
- Financial Capability
- Dominant Buying Motive

To sell effectively you must gain insight into these five areas with any prospect. You gain insight through the intelligent use of questions.

While it may be possible to gain three pieces of information from one question, it is often possible to gather 25 pieces of information from five questions.

Two types of questions:

Closed questions ask a prospect for answers in very specific areas and do not call for much flexibility. These questions are called "closed" because the possible answers fall with a few options, which are limited to very few possibilities. Typically the answer to a closed question is either "yes" or "no".

Open questions ask a prospect to respond with any answer from within a broad, perhaps unlimited range of answers. Open questions do not attempt to structure or limit a prospect's response.

Knowing which mode of question to use to determine different categories of information can be a great advantage in securing needed information.

Open questions encourage prospects to respond freely. Here are a few examples of open questions:
"What was the last supplier like?"

"If you could change one thing about these features what would that be?"
"How have the products serviced your needs?"
"Tell me about the pressures you face in this department."
"Who would be the best person to talk to and why?"

Close questions limit the possible answers to questions. Generally, they must be answered by a "yes" or a "no" or a very specific or brief answer. Here a few examples of closed questions:
"Have you ever thought of bringing in a supplier like us?"
"Has this program ever failed you?"
Keep in mind that open questions generally are useful for getting more insight into a prospect's feeling, perceptions and expectations. Closed questions are more useful for direction the conversation and confirming understanding of either yourself or the prospect.

Relationships

In today's environment the relationship with the client is critical.

If you have done your job well, you have worked on installing rapport; the customer feels comfortable with you and is ready to proceed in the buying cycle. You have listened well and done a thorough investigation. Rather than talking, you realise that listening is much better than talking. You could not present information yet without the prospect's input. You feel that the customer has received a "Yes" answer to the question he is asking him/herself which at this point in the sale is, "Do they (the salespeople) understand my needs?"

You then present solutions to the client. You now know what the customer wants and needs, what they can afford and what their buying motive is, so you are ready to present your solutions. Still remember that listening is always the best approach. You then deal with the prospect's concerns. By doing a solid presentation you will have alleviated most of the concerns the prospect had. They will never approve the sale and commit to you unless they get a "Yes" answer to the question. Once you have successfully met their concerns, closing is a natural outcome of a proper sales job.

Don't be nervous, forget all the stupid tricks and assume the sale.
It's not that those tricks don't work, unfortunately they do sometimes. But in today's environment, the relationship is primary.

Referrals are the way of choice for us now. If you have to use tricks to close sales, you

might succeed once but you can forget about
the long term.

Remember, we must never do anything to
jeopardize trust and customer referrals.

Chapter 11

Get a Winning Attitude

Monday: Another big sale went to your competition. It looked so sure.

Tuesday: Three times today you hear "No, I don't need a new supplier."

Wednesday: You get call from a client who informs you that a sale is cancelled.

Thursday: After 20 rejections in a row you are asking yourself, "Why am I in sales?"

Friday: You procrastinate and kill time for two hours instead of making those cold calls you know you should be making.

Have you ever wondered how some people just seem to be highly motivated most of the time? Why, are they positive even in the face of disappointments and frustrations? What can be done to keep your circumstances from affecting your attitude?

Is it possible to stay motivated? What do those "positive thinkers" actually do to stay that way?

Below are three ways to get and keep a Winning Attitude.

1. Control the Self-Talk

Stop everything, when you start hearing yourself saying things like "I can't", "I'm not smart enough", "It's too hard", "I'm not good at selling,".....any time you hear negative self talk, Stop It.

When you are about to make some of those dreaded "cold calls", call them "gold calls". You are in control. You have the ability to confront your feelings. Exercise command of what you say to yourself.

2. Beware of Your Limiting Belief Systems

The first step to growth is awareness. One of the best things you can be aware of is any limiting beliefs you have about yourself. Read through this list. Using the following scale, rate yourself.

Which one or two areas tend to be your major struggling points?

U = Usually
S = Sometimes
R = Rarely

- fears change
- fears rejection
- is critical of self
- is easily discouraged
- is preoccupied with past
- is defensive
- talks negatively of self
- lacks decisiveness
- is critical of others
- tends to question self compares self with others.
- fears failure
- always pessimistic
- feels inadequate
- has difficulty establishing meaningful relationships
- attempts to control others to make self look good
- feels self-conscious
- worries about what others think
- needs continual approval
- is insecure around others
- takes things personally

Do you detect any areas which may be responsible for a limiting belief system? Identify the two most pronounced items and begin working on those first.

At one point in my life, I would have answered "Usually" to almost every one of those questions. I have learned how much limiting belief is harmful to my success.

Today, I am enjoying a level of success and happiness I never dreamed possible, all because I became aware of the weak links in my belief system and was willing to take some risks in those areas and grow.

3. Reprogram Negative Mental Types

Once you have decided to assume responsibility for the outcome of your life and discovered any limiting beliefs about yourself, now you are ready to erase the negative thoughts we often play inside our mind.

Society, family, friends, economies, school, and sometimes even religion have programmed you to think a whole lot less about yourself than you should.

The process of clearing and reproducing those mental thoughts are not easy

You should use power statements like, "I am a worthwhile person, no matter what you think of me or say to me."

<u>Helpful Power Statements</u>
I am lovable and capable
I am confident
I am enthusiastic
I am a success
I take risks
I will not quit
I am a winner
I love myself
People love me

Practice these three rules and you will have a Winner's attitude and things will turn around.

Monday: You are pumped up ready to tackle the week.

Tuesday: You keep your great attitude despite being turned down four times in a row.

Wednesday: You listen to podcasts on positive thinking and you have an incredible amount of energy to start calling those prospects.

Thursday: Another terrible blow from head office, a price increase, you start practising controlling what you say to yourself. You are feeling okay even with the bad news.

Friday: A pile of people want to do business with you. Your attitude is contagious. Your attitude is contagious. You have discovered the keys to attracting success.

Chapter 12

Build a Powerful Sales Team

If you have a dynamic, powerful sales force, you are indeed lucky. But maybe luck has little to do with it. If you have a sales team of powerhouse players then you must be doing something right.

The old adage of, 20 percent of your salespeople give you 80 percent of your sales holds true. Some managers even report that today, in some companies a 10 percent / 90 percent ratio is closer to reality.

Those percentages are terrible. It costs you too much money to maintain that kind of failure rate. How can we improve our odds in sales management?

Guidelines for Effective Sales Management

Make sure that the new recruits never hit the street until they are totally sold on your product or service. They must be as excited about what they are selling as you are.

Demand 100 percent commitment from them. They must be ready to do whatever it takes to win, to perform at maximum capacity from the word – go. They must be focused on the customer only. Listening must be their primary task with a view to long-term relationships.

They should be mentored by your top salespeople. They should always have access to you and to your staff. You must pay more than lip-service to sales training. Ensure that they are learning the leading-edge techniques on prospecting, including direct marketing techniques.

They must be learning powerful probing skills, rapport and trust building. They need to know how to handle all the objections in your industry. They need several powerful methods to get the order, close the sale.

They must see you at your best, always. That includes your dress, your attitude, your dealing with others; like never speaking negatively behind the back of another salesperson.

You must teach them the importance of attitude management. They must develop the top methods for snapping back from a bad sales call. They must learn how to incorporate humour into their daily lives.

Push Their Emotional Triggers

Not every technique will work for everyone. Even the least experienced manager will know that what works for one person might not work for another. One sales person will not respond the same way another does. One may like the motivational talks but another is pumped up with the sales contest that allows them to become more productive because of their emotional trigger of financial incentive.

Find Everyone's Emotional Triggers

Here are a few triggers I have discovered:

- **Recognition**: This trigger is pretty obvious to detect. This person craves applause. They love to be seen as successful. They usually drive the more expensive car. They wear the fancy jewellery and stylish clothes. They must be noticed, so take notice.
- **Power**: This trigger is seen in how much a person is willing to expand to influence a situation. This trigger appeals to the person's sense of wanting authority. They want to be in charge and dislike loss of control.
- **Safety**: This trigger is fostered by a need to be secure. It is usually focussed on the future and making things safe.
- **Status**: Similar to Recognition, this emotional trigger seeks those status

symbols that let others know they have arrived. They hate being part of the crowd. They don't want to buy, use, or win anything that is available to others. They are into being unique.

- **Relationships**: Some people are into being friends. This is most obvious in their need to be reassured that they matter. They want to know that they are needed, appreciated, trusted, enjoyed and generally liked. They are often perceived as needing a hug. They want acceptance.

Guidelines to Successful Recruiting

Always be on the lookout. There is never a time when you aren't available to sell someone on joining your team. Tell others that you are always looking to help someone become rich.

Get your existing salespeople enrolled to helping you find good people. Consider paying them for recommending the right person. Hire only people who absolutely are in love with selling. Offer more training than your competition offers.

Give your salespeople what they want. Some want money, some want recognition, some want education, some want opportunity for advancement. Give them what they want.

Know what you are looking for and what type of person will fit your corporate culture. Get your existing, salespeople involved in the selection process. Have them meet your prospective recruit. Then have them send personal notes stating that they would love to work with them.

What to Look For In a Sales Recruit

Look for someone who is:

- Attractive
- Well-dressed
- Willing to learn
- Hungry to succeed
- A people person
- Extrovert
- Wants to make a lot of money
- Willing to do whatever it takes
- Optimistic
- Thinks big
- Ambitious
- Entrepreneurial
- A creative problem-solver
- Self-confident and not afraid to work hard
- Balanced in his/her personal life
- Somewhat rebellious and not a crowd-follower
- Self-disciplined.

Find this kind of person and you are on your way to building a solid team. Find several of these types and you are on your way to sales management stardom.

Rules for Being a Good Sales Manager

- Demand 100 percent from yourself
- Be the best you can be
- Develop a reputation as a person who is personally self-disciplined. This will win you respect
- Build self-confidence
- Be a learner. Always attend seminars, read, listen to positive medias
- Look for people who are better at selling than you. Get confident and secure enough to find smarter, more attractive, more skilled people
- Really care for your people
- Ask more than telling
- Always be on the lookout to recruit solid, talented salespeople
- Don't be harsh. Build on their strengths
- Find out what their goals are and help them keep those goals in focus. Help them get those goals
- Help them deal with lost sales and failures by taking every thought captive
- Evaluate specific behaviours not vague generalities
- Give them personal attention. Send personal notes to them.
- Smile more

- Remind them that you are there to help them
- Never be defensive
- Encourage them to share their challenges with you
- Show respect
- Give them incentives for top performance
- Praise them individually in public more
- Learn and teach them more effective prospecting skills.
- Have more uplifting sales meetings.
- Teach them to deal with rejection
- Remember that you can't listen and talk at the same time

Chapter 13

99 Great Sales Strategies

To win at sales, you must have two things: You must have *effective* strategies and you must act *consistently* on those strategies. Below are 99 different sales strategies I have used, taught or heard about over my many years in the sales trenches.

1. **Listen**: You have one mouth and two ears. Listen twice as much as you talk.

2. **Stay in Touch**: Make a decision to contact all your past clients at least once a month. If you don't, guess what? Your competition will.

3. **Differentiate Yourself**: Why should someone buy from you? What makes you different from everyone else? You should be more significant than your competitor.

4. **Ignore the Competition**: If you are looking at them or worried about them at all, your focus is in the wrong direction. You should make dealing with you so much more powerful that competition doesn't even exist.

5. **Control Your Mind**: Whatever helps you stay positive is what you need to do first thing in the morning and the last thing you do before you see a prospect. For me it's loud music. I put on a good song and my adrenaline starts to flow.

6. **Get Rid of Negative People From Your Life**: Now, that might be somewhat difficult if you are married to them, and I am not advocating divorce but you need to surround yourself with a solid group of positive, big thinking encouragers.

7. **Send Out 35 Prospecting Emails Every Week**: Get in the habit of sending out at least that many emails to prospects every week. No matter what, make sure they go out every week.

8. **Get a CRM System**: Do you know how much moneymaking time you waste trying to remember who your prospects are and when was the last time you called them? If you want to make more money, get properly organized.

9. **Think Big**: You must see the potential within you. Someone once told me that my yearly income (low six figures at the time) was garbage. "Garbage?" Yes, it's garbage for you to

make that much a year when you have the potential to earn that much in a month! I had never entertained the idea that I could. I did it. Now, I am working on how I can do that much in a day. (Once I figure that one out I'll let you know, then I'll figure out how to do it in an hour!)

10. **Learn From Your Mistakes**: Every sales job has some "failure factor" in it. Learn from it and keep on going.

11. **Stop "Trying"**: Trying to do something is a cop out. Either, do it, or don't, but stop lying to yourself.

12. **Create Special Offers**: No matter what you sell, you can create a special offer which will put you in a favourable light in the eyes of prospects.

13. **Write a Special Report**: If you are in selling, you are solving. What do you solve for people? Write a 10 page report, offer it to your prospects for free and your phone will ring.

14. **Give up Manipulation Tricks**: Stop using those silly closing tricks you learned about to make the buyer buy. Instead, listen to your clients, build trust and they will buy.

15. **Put Your Message on Video**: Put your entire sales presentation on video, You Tube or a free webinar and prospects will see that you are different from the competition.

16. **Use Contact Cards**: A contact card is a postcard that is printed on both sides. One side has your picture "A Note From..." and your contact information. Keep 20 of them on you always with postage stamps already on them. After each sales call, write a quick thank you note to your prospect, drop it in the mail box. You will create a positive impression.

17. **Write a U.S.P.**: A U.S.P. stands for Unique Selling Proposition. What is your number one competitive selling advantage? It should be brief, exciting and should compel people to want to know more.

18. **Realise That Your Past Clients are Gold**: You will starve if you have to continue to find new customers. Repackage what you sell and visit them again and again and again.

19. **Make a Deal with Your Competitors**: Do you have prospects that you have been unable to sell? Why not go to a competitor and let them have a try. They might be able to sell people you were unable to and pay

you part of what they make. You do the same for their list of dead prospects.

20. **Deliver Fast**: Society is impatient. People will not put up with slow delivery.

21. **Got Nuts With Follow-up**: I'm serious, you will never offend someone by sending a thank you note. It will tell them you value the relationship.

22. **Think Long-Term**: If you are in it for the one time sale, you will be hungry and poor in this business. Everything you do should be focussed on keeping this customer happy for the next 20 years.

23. **Be Confident**: If you have confidence in yourself, your product, your company, prospects will have confidence in you. If they have confidence in you they are much more likely to buy from you.

24. **Get Related Quickly**: Establish rapport with prospects quickly by finding something that relates the two of you. It could be a hobby, a common interest, children, but find something.

25. **Ask More Questions**: People want to know that you understand what

they are going through. Why not ask twice as many questions on your next sales call and see what happens.

26. **Become a Single Figure**: Remember that selling is more about perception than about products. Get interviewed, write a book, booklet or report. Produce a video, give a speech. Become known.

27. **Get Your Customers to Own You**: If you sell insurance, make sure that when they think of insurance they think of you. If you sell real estate ensure they automatically think of you.

28. **Use the Power of Because**: Every time you talk about or describe a benefit to your prospect for what you sell, be sure to tell them why that is important to them.

29. **Do what's Right**: Don't do what you think is right. Do what the prospect thinks is right. There is only one way to find that out and that's to ask, test and measure.

30. **Keep Your Customers Happy at All Costs**: If you fail in this area, you will fail to build the greatest assets in the sales world and that is a client base that trusts you.

31. **Develop and Keep a Positive Attitude**: I know of very few statues erected to "cynics and critics". Get happy, read a good book or listen to an inspiring message.

32. **Be Professional**: Forget about begging for business.

33. **Move On**: When cold calling, if you encounter someone who tries to make you feel bad, simply thank them for their time and move on.

34. **Sell to Help**: People don't care how much you know until they know how much you care. Get your eyes off your commission and onto their problems.

35. **Sell At Your Location**: There is something called "home court advantage." Get them to come to you if possible.

36. **Break One Bad Habit Today**: Pick one thing you know you should stop doing (drinking, smoking, coffee, snacks, etc) and decide to stop one thing. Get someone to hold you accountable, give them your plan and break it, finally and forever.

37. **List 10 Things you Like About Yourself**: Work on building your self-esteem. Sometimes it's so easy to

focus on all our flaws. Give yourself a break today.

38. **Set a Goal for the Year**: What's one thing you would really like to accomplish in your selling this year? Write it on a small card and carry it with you wherever you go.

39. **Attract Prospects by Conducting a Seminar**: This is a great way for you to have people who are in the market to buy what you sell step forward and identify themselves. Why would you ever want to sell one person at a time when you could sell to several?

40. **Be Unique**: Do something different. Send people a dead flower and tell them that you can bring flowers back to life with a special potion, all they have to do to find out how, is book an appointment with you.

41. **Get Funny**: So many people are so uptight. Relax, let your hair down. It is a powerful sales tool. Humour can do for you in seconds what talking wouldn't do in a lifetime.

42. **Use Testimonials**: One of the most powerful tools you can have is the endorsements from satisfied clients.

43. **Use Pictures**: Pictures of satisfied clients go further than lengthy emails. People are visual and if they see people just like them, they will think you are okay.

44. **Create Your Own Marketing Binder**: Put any awards you have in the binder along with photos, testimonial, product information, how you do business, your sales presentation and leave it with prospects, so they can evaluate you.

45. **Be Prompt**: When you make someone wait, it communicates lack of respect for their time. Be respectful and it will help your image.

46. **Find The Real Objection**: Clients may not always feel comfortable telling you the number problem at first.

47. **Be Honest**: I once caught a car salesperson in a lie. I shut them down immediately. People want to buy from people they can trust.

48. **Raise Your Referral Rates**: Research shows that the average salesperson gets less than 10 per cent of their income from referrals. This is not acceptable.

49. **Don't Do Administration During Prime Selling Time**: What are you doing at your desk that is more important than being in front of prospects?

50. **Stop Cold Calling**: Get them coming to you. You can't kiss someone who is backing away from you. Give the client some compelling reason to come to you. A clue: the word FREE is still one of the most loved words.

51. **Welcome Complaints**: You can turn around most complaints if you are committed to winning. Make it easy and acceptable for them to tell you how they feel about you.

52. **Create Urgency**: Every email, every sales call, every marketing piece must have a deadline.

53. **Sell Your Guarantee**: If you have a guarantee, tell your prospects about it. Too many guarantees are full of small print and so salespeople never get the advantage they were intended to create.

54. **Ask for the Order**: This simple advice should be obvious.

55. **Don't Be a Door Mat**: If people are putting you or your company down, stand up to them. You should have

pride. You don't need any customer that much.

56. **Save 10 Per Cent of Everything You Earn**: Starting with your next pay check, put 10 per cent away for yourself. Why is it that we pay everyone else but ourselves?

57. **Join Toastmasters**: They will teach you how to speak in public. The benefits of that are tremendous for your sales presentation and confidence. You can find their information online.

58. **Refuse to Quit**: You will never win in selling if you give up. I have felt like stopping about a million times but I know that I'll never learn anything from giving up except how to quit.

59. **Take Responsibility for Your Results**: You are the only person who can improve your situation. You got yourself into it and you are the one who will get yourself out.

60. **Sponsor a Community Event**: Give back to your community and they will give back to you.

61. **Instead of an Email letter, Send an Audio Clip**: Instead of writing a standard email, speak your message into an audio clip and separate

yourself from the other emails they are receiving that day.

62. **Get on Everyone's Mailing List**: I love to learn from what people send me.

63. **Get Your Spending in Line**: Credit can kill you. If you are consistently spending more than you are earning you are in for a bad time. Trust me, get rid of the credit cards, and cut back your expense. You can't sell well if you are worried about debt.

64. **Use a Headline in Your Sales Letters**: Also keep in mind that every sales letter must have a P.S. You have less than five seconds to capture their interest, headline and P.S.'s help.

65. **Sponsor a Contest**: This will give you a vehicle to build your database in a hurry.

66. **Record an Interview**: Get a friend with the best voice to ask you a series of questions and record it on audio. Then give it away to prospects. Title it *An Interview with.....*

67. **If Possible Charge Differently than Others**: Make comparison shopping difficult.

68. **Clean up Your Life**: Everyone has certain things they procrastinate

about. If you have been planning to clean that desk of yours and it's getting in the way of you increasing your product, clean it up.

69. **Qualify First**: Don't start selling until you have enough information about what they need.

70. **Assume Prospects are NOT Liars**: Most salespeople I know think that prospects are liars and will do just about anything rather than give you the truth. I assume they tell me the truth until they give me some reason to not believe that.

71. **Use the Phone to Weed People out, Not Prospect**: Use the phone to disqualify non-buyers.

72. **Create Order in Your Client Base**: You should have a list of all your past contacts, past clients, hot prospects in an easy to use database.

73. **Position Yourself as an "Expert and Authority"**: Even if you are new to your industry you can be perceived as an expert. The way to do it is with information. Write something, research something or print something and you are an instant "expert".

74. **Get in Front of the Right Person or Don't Waste Your Time**: So many salespeople complain about not closing more sales but they spend forever trying to sell to the wrong people. If the decision maker is the VP of Production then you stop talking to the VP of Human Resources. Figure how to get to the right person.

75. **Under Pressure?** Take a day off.

76. **Use Cross Promotions**: Find someone who is in front of your target market and get them to send a compelling offer to their client base.

77. **Build, Manage and Exploit Your Database**: Your list of contacts is one of the most valuable assets you have. Always add more names to it. Get them coming to you by regularly creating offers that make them step forward. Get everyone's contact information.

78. **Get Rid of Hassle Rules**: If you can, get rid of all negative rules your company has, like "No refunds without receipt" or "No cheque accepted."

79. **Blow Your Customers Away by Exceeding Their Expectations**: The word of mouth benefits of doing this is fabulous.

80. **Build a Wall Of Fame**: In your office create a wall for all letters of praise and endorsements.

81. **Give Something Away**: People love getting Free Samples, Free Offers, Reports, Booklets, DVD's, etc.

82. **Host an Annual Special Event for Your Past Clients**: Want more referrals? Why not host a party, social, seminar, forum twice a year and only invite your past clients?

83. **Focus on the Customer Not on You**: People don't care about you, your credentials, or your company. They only care about one thing: Themselves. More specifically, how spending their hard-earned money will solve their problems?

84. **Snap to it**: Take your past client's picture and send it to them.

85. **Keep in Touch**: Send a weekly or monthly report or newsletter via email. Send a positive quotation of the day.

86. **Start Your Own Association**: A.A.R.P. is the American Association for Retired People. It has 30 million members. Guess who started it? An insurance company who wanted to sell to retired people.

87. **Write a Book**: If you knew what a book would do for you and your sales, you'd be up for the next month writing it and it would be done. Give yourself permission and reap the benefits.

88. **Print a Personal Brochure**: Even if your company has a corporate brochure, create one on You. People don't buy from companies they buy from people. This will set you apart from the competition.

89. **Increase the Size of Each Sale**: Ask for bigger orders.

90. **Invest in Yourself**: Get the best books, check out webinars, get a support system. Spend money on training yourself.

91. **Be a Person of Integrity**: Be a person your kids would be happy to emulate.

92. **Take a Break**: When was the last time you kissed your spouse? When was the last time you gave yourself fully to your kids?

93. **Focus on The Journey Not the Prize**: Selling is about becoming a better person. It's not really about hitting the home run. Sure that's important but what is more important

are all the wonderful ways you are better because you are a professional salesperson.

94. **Target a Lot**: Everyone may not be a good prospect for your products or services. But your targeted marketing strategies will produce the best results for that will surely save you money and time. Customize your marketing materials to appeal to their greatest need.

95. **Keep Trying**: Keep trying, keep improving, keep testing and evaluating the effectiveness of all your marketing strategies that you use or do to promote your business. Before you know it you will be able to easily identify what has helped your business grow, and what has not.

96. **Take a Few Minutes**: Take a few minutes to evaluate how well you're implementing each marketing strategy into your business. Even a small improvement in just one area will help boost your sales revenue immediately.

97. **Treat Your Weaknesses as Strengths**. Customers may not know your firm (a weakness) but they don't have negative preconceptions either (a strength).

98. **Be Your Firm's Greatest Strength.** Top executives don't have the time to sit with down with cookie-cutter salespeople, but they always have time for somebody who can redefine problems and devise solutions. If you can truly add value, you're the most valuable person that CEO will meet with that day, maybe that month, maybe even that year.

99. **Think Like an Entrepreneur.** If your firm lacks the infrastructure of a larger firm, the only person you can trust to get things done is YOU. Be frugal with your time and resources, and constantly find creative ways to get things done more quickly and easily.

If you can take even a few of these proven sales strategies and make them a part of your regular sales process, you will be surprised at how quickly the results will follow.

Chapter 14

Common Selling Quotations

Some quotations are good, some are bad. Let's look at a few to see which ones we, as salespeople, should embrace and which ones we should discard.

"Fake it till you make it."

Fake it? Fake what? Is "fake" something you want to be associated with? I want to be genuine. I think we should re-word it to "Be genuine at all costs."

People want to buy from someone they trust. If you don't have that trust you can forget the sale, repeat business and most importantly, referrals. Let nothing about you resemble being fake. Be real, be honest, be yourself. If your heart is in the right place there's no need to mask anything. You can't "fake" your heart.

"Selling is a numbers game."

Unfortunately many people look at selling that way. This quotation stems from the idea that if you knock on 100 doors or are rejected 99 times you will find one buyer. So in the sense, I guess selling is a number game.

Is it the game you want to play? Do you like the odd numbers? The reason those numbers are so terrible is that salespeople are chasing "unqualified, disinterested prospects." Their reward for that is untold misery caused by constant rejection.

Sure, selling might be a numbers game. Do what I do. I figure out how to make the biggest number of my market come to me, call me or in some way approach me. I attract them like magnets, and in big numbers. If anyone is doing rejecting is should be you.

"Every 'No' leads you closer to a 'Yes'."

Being similar to the other quotation, this one tries to brain-wash people into liking being rejected. I've heard some bright motivational gurus tell people to see each the word "No" as $5 in the bank because you are that much closer to a "Yes."

You will never convince me that you can

make salespeople immune to rejection. A "No" is a "No" is a "No". It isn't pretty, no matter how many mental gymnastics you use to make it less painful.

This nonsense is one of the reasons most salespeople toil away, day in and day out in an approach to selling which is ineffective. They never consider how to figure out how to sell with rejection.

"Fail to plan and plan to fail."

There's one we should follow. So often, poor performers are disorganised and their desk is messy, they don't return calls, they miss appointments. I know of one person who drove across town and realised his presentation folder was still on his desk. The tragedy was that this was the second time this happened; with the same client. It might be as simple as taking five minutes before you go to bed to focus yourself for the next day but without a plan you are doomed.

"To be enthusiastic, act enthusiastic."

I like this. So often when I get tired and I notice my energy levels start to weaken. I sit up straight. I change my breathing. I clap my hands, make some noise. Maybe I'll listen to some good music. Someone said that motion creates emotion. Moving yourself around when you want more enthusiasm helps.

"People don't care how much you know until they know how much you care."

Focus on the client, not on your commission. That will take care of itself if you put the prospect first.

"Sell, sell, sell, and all will be well."

This is the number one focus in our profession. It doesn't say "Sell, sell, sell at any cost." It says that most of your sales problems will be fixed once you sell, sell, sell. It is possible for you to sell more. Figure out how. Move into action. Get accountable.

So many of the top income earners in selling are some of the most committed people to self development.

"Just ask for order."

In many cases you would be making a big mistake to ask for the order. There is only one time you should ask for the order and that is when the client has given you ample evidence that they are sold. This requires that you listen for buying signals. If you ask for the order too soon, you'll scare them away.

"There are no problems in life, only a shortage of ideas"

This is a great philosophy of life. Most people are locked into their problems. All they can see is what's not working out. They are so focused on the problems that they never see the opportunities.

They cannot see opportunities because the minute you get lost in the problem your creative juices stop flowing. So the next time you are faced with a mountain of problems, concentrate on this quotation. You are only one idea away from solving this problem.

Chapter 15

How to Keep Customers for Life

It happens so often. Work forever to find and sell a client, then lose them. Has this ever happened to you?

You work with a prospect only to find out that at the last minute, they bought from your competitor. A company you know had a higher price than you.

You make a call to a long-standing client, and they tell you they are no longer in the market to buy what you are selling.

All of a sudden, a trusted referral base dries up for you. The person who referred many prospects to you suddenly fails to return your calls and stops sending people to you.

What happened? Can this sort of thing be prevented? Is it possible to ensure that the hard work you did to find and sell people, continues? Is it possible to prevent your prospects and customers from going to the competitor? It most certainly is possible and essential to continue to sell effectively.

Keep in mind how vital this role in selling really is. Most of your energy, time and expense are in the "locating" of prospects and client bases. You spend most of your time trying to find hot prospects and sell them. You feel wonderful once you sell them but what about after that? Unless you change this aspect of your selling career, you are doomed to spend forever on the sales roller-coaster.

Understand Your Client Base

One of the first things to do when you work for a company is to get them to define their client base. Your client base is probably the most valuable asset you own. So many salespeople fail to even organize it, let alone define it.

With the advantage of technology there is no excuse for salespeople not to have an extensive database. At the very least you need to have a well though-out system for managing your client base.

It's been so long that you have been in contact with your past clients that some of them have moved, moved out of the country, or died and you have no way of knowing because you are in contact with them so infrequently.

The first thing you should do is to list everyone in your client base and confirm that that information you have is correct. Contact everyone by phone or email. If possible, set up a personal interview with everyone. The referral potential alone by doing this can be of great benefit. Now divide all the names into one of three networks.

The Three Networks

Everyone you come into contact with, will fall into one of these three networks. Each one should have a different strategy of contact management and each one should be kept separately. Thinking about your client base in these three networks will allow you to be very organized and thorough in your planning and it will ensure that no one slips through the cracks.

Everyone in your client base should receive high priority or don't have them in there. The following system calls for different strategies for each category.

- **The Established Network**
  The Established Network is composed of past clients, current clients and your top producing clients. These people are known to you and you are

known to them. You have an established relationship with them.

- **The Prospect Network**
  The Prospect Network is composed of new prospects. The idea is to use attraction as the primary marketing tool. The goal with this network is to stay in constant contact with them so that when they are ready to buy, you will know it and they will naturally think of you.

- **The Specialty Network**
  This network is often neglected by most salespeople. Every industry has a specialty network. It could be corporate accounts, governmental contacts or associations.

Anyone who has a special relationship with you in the sense that they can send many people your way should be part of this network.

If you are a real estate agent, then a mortgage broker, lawyer or accountant might be a multiple source contact. It would make sense then to have several of these in your specialty network and prospect for them. These are people who are in front of a large number of people who are pre-disposed to buy what you are selling.

Determine How Much Contact Is Ideal

It is long been established that the more
frequently a prospect, referrer, or past client
hears from you the more likely they are to
buy from you, refer others to you or re-order
from you. So why don't more salespeople
stay in contact with them?

Chasing the Best Customer

The old way of selling says that to win you
have to find the next customer. People have
been taught that to win at selling you must
be out there cold calling in the marketplace.
We would all agree that 20 per cent of the
people will give us 80 per cent of the
business. Conversely, 80 per cent of the
people will give us only 20 per cent of our
sales.
The 20 per cent is what is called the known
market and the 80 per cent is the unknown
market. Past clients, hot prospects and
specialty networks are all the part of the
known market. You need to spend more time
here.

If you do your job well in building a solid
relationship with your client, based on trust,
honesty, integrity and frequency, you will
have them for life. The biggest expense in
any business is the cost of client acquisition,
so once you acquire a client it makes good
economic sense to do everything in your

power to make each person in your client base a top priority.

Frequency is the Key

What usually happens, is that salespeople will send out a holiday card, maybe a birthday card and be in touch with their client base when they have time. With clients, it is better to have too much frequency rather than too little.
Here are some guidelines for better contact management and client retention:

Be unique
Make sure that every time you make contact with your client base, that it is different. Doing something different could mean sending out Christmas cards one month early and joke about how organized you are.

Focus on them
The idea of contacting people only looking for business will be counter productive. Instead, focus on them. Focus on building the relationship. Use humour if appropriate.

Position for referrals
If you sell houses, why not take a photo of the best listing of the month and email a photo to your entire client base every month. They may know someone who could buy it.

Do it often
I recommend that you have a strategic plan

for each network. Each one should be contacted according to a well thought-out plan. To assist you with this, you could utilize someone in your office to address envelopes and cards for one afternoon a week. This could be the best thing you ever do for your sales career.

The Established Network – contact at least 24 times per year.

The Prospect Network – contact at least 12 times per year.

The Specialty Network – contact no less than 12 times per year.

This may cause you to radically change your priorities in selling. If you are not making the money you know you can make in selling and you are working very hard, the reason could be that you are chasing the unknown and neglecting the known Market. Change your focus.

Reason To Contact

Here are some reasons to contact your network:

Irresistible Offers:
Why not re-package what you sell and give them an irresistible offer. I know of an insurance agent who sent all of his clients a

postcard with how much coverage they had and he offered and additional $100,000 of coverage for a small monthly fee. All they had to do to get it was place a checkmark on the postcard and send it back. The response was outstanding.

Provide Desired Information
Consider becoming a source of information for people. Whenever you have new information, it gives you a natural "in" to contact them. Find out what information you can supply on an on-going basis for your client base.

Special Events
Think about the value of having an annual celebration for everyone in your client base. I know of a real estate agent who holds an annual dance on Valentines Day. She picks this date because the best months for real estate are April to June, right after her big event. Her name is fresh in the minds of all of her clients.

Chapter 16

Entrepreneurial Economy

Worldwide pressures and trends are forcing a major reorganization of many sales and bureaucratic organizations. Companies are striving to cut costs, streamline their operations and replace people with more technology.

These effects are already being felt by many people today. Leaders in all sectors who are unable to cope with these changes will be forced into dangerous territory. The effective way to win in the next few years will be to identify the entrepreneurial trends and master the strategies that will remain valid over the next decade regardless of the changes that will take place in the market place.

Thriving in the next decade

For many people whose hopes and dreams are based on entrepreneurial risk taking, this will be a wonderful time to be alive. It will be the greatest period of entrepreneurial opportunity in history. It will be a time filled with excitement, creativity, success and satisfaction.

I have identified some of the trends I see as vital to be aware of, in order to thrive in the next decade and also some corresponding strategies that can ensure personal and corporate health. These trends are vital for long-term planning, but also important to salespeople who want to remain on the cutting edge of innovation.

Focus on goals rather than on results.

This trend is not new. It is however vital for us to consider, particularly as we entertain innovative ideas and methodologies. There is a tendency for people to direct their energies to their present results rather than on their goals.

In addition to the obvious benefits to focusing on goals, we also see a strength in those individuals who have the ability to keep on track even when everything around them seems chaotic. The salespeople or organizations that focus on well thought out goals will be able to survive the upheaval of the economy.

Focus on attraction rather than rejection

The old cold calling approach of selling is gone. Only those who are willing to consider a new approach will survive in the next decade. The organizations and individuals who can somehow attract the right type of prospects will have a much better change to gain market share.

Most organizations focus almost exclusively in chasing "new" business. I would much rather focus in on selling those people and companies which are "known" to me. The notion of knocking on 100 doors to find the one who will buy is outdated.

The problem most organizations and salespeople face is the shortage of hot prospects. Most people are using the needle in the haystack approach. Keep searching, searching, and searching for someone who "might" buy instead of attracting a constant flow of people who are predisposed to buy what you sell.

There is no such thing as call reluctance when you have to call someone back who has called you first. There are many possibilities for attracting your target market. If you know exactly "who" you are targeting, if you know where they hurt and you talk about how you can solve their problems then you can make the one's who are most likely to buy from you - call you. Just imagine how great you would feel today if you had 300 leads to follow up of people who called you looking for more information.

What will attract them?
An event - seminars, forums, discussions, parties, VIP events, private meeting.
An offer - free anything, related to what you sell will make them come out of the woodwork.
An interesting problem-solving solution.
Information - people are starving for information, provide it and they will come to you.

Focus on relationships

The money is in relationships.

Bill Gates and Steve Jobs think about the long-term, not the short-term. They are not interested in selling you gadgets, computer software or applications, they want to sell it to your kids and their kids and their kids' kids. They are focused on the "forever" not the "now".

The entrepreneurial economy that is emerging will direct you to a "marriage" model rather than a "one-night stand" model of selling.

When it comes to sales and marketing, the problem is that sometimes the "one night stand" approach works. But the real money is in the "marriage" model. If you are selling and not communicating regularly with your past clients, if you are selling and not nurturing the long-term relationship, then you are using the wrong approach. In the next decade, this is one of the surest ways to sales poverty. Get committed to the "forever".

Develop loyalty and avoid loss of loyalty

Loyalty is developed by regular, customer contact. The fastest way to ensure loss of loyalty from the client base you have is to provide infrequent contact which is primarily focused on you instead of them.

Loyalty is to sales success as fuel is to driving a car.

You cannot have one without the other. Do you have clients that you have not contacted in the past six months? When you contact them, are you simply trying to get a referral, another sale? You cannot have a good marriage which only focused on "getting".

Another key point to keep in mind is that people don't care about you. They care about themselves, their problems, fears, desires, challenges and obstacles. So why do you contact them so infrequently and when you do, you focus on the thing they are least interested in...You.

Why not try finding out what they need, what interests them, what motivates them and let that be the focus of your communications with them? Why not send them articles, magazines, etc...

and develop the relationship to the point that they are loyal to you.

Make use of multiple marketing vehicles

Consider using some unique, alternative marketing ideas. Why not create a personal brochure for yourself? Why not hold a seminar to attract prospects? Join Toastmasters, a non-profit worldwide organization which will help you develop your public speaking skills? You could write a book or booklet, or a special report. Produce a monthly audio newsletter and talk about the trends in your industry and review a book and offer it for free to prospects?

Why not send out postcards, with a catchy headline stating some impressive benefit for calling you. What if you sent out 100 cards offering a free Special Report? You would have more leads than you know what to do with.

Focus on Being Different

One of the fastest ways to gain huge strides quickly is to be different than everyone else who sells what you sell, including people from within your own company.

It is not easy to stand out from the crowd, but being different will help.

Focus on money-making activities

You don't get a commission for surfing the web. You don't make money by staying in the office, working on reports and filling out forms. While some of that is important, why do you do it during prime selling time? Why don't you utilize someone in the office or hire someone part-time to work one or two afternoons or evenings?

If you earned $50,000 last year and you did that with only 15 per cent of your time on money-making time, imagine what would happen to your income if you increased your money-making time to 40 per cent? Think what this means.

Get out of your office and go find a client!

Chapter 17

Dating vs. Marriage

What do most people do in a cold call situation? They call someone out of the blue and basically ask for a date. "You don't know me, but I'm really good, do you want to get married?"

Married? This is essentially the question you are asking your prospects. This is a really big step for a prospect and they usually respond with a "Not interested." The vast majority of your prospects will typically respond this way based on your approach.

Many business owners, Presidents, VP's, sales managers, push their people to close more business. They usually don't want to wait for it to happen either. The pressure is on you to close more prospects. So you engage in uncomfortable behaviour that you may not be very successful at. This can often cause you to approach your job with less than stellar motivation.

So how should you date?

What would happen if you asked your prospect how they would like to date? Now don't take me literally. What would your first step be? How about getting opt-in that your prospect would even be interested in hearing from you? That will take some skilful positioning of the right message, to the right target audience, using the right marketing channels. This will allow you to attract instead of chase.

What if you started asking better questions to your prospects to show your expertise without bragging about how great you are? Everyone is always a rock star in their own minds, but the way you conduct yourself tells the real story. Besides, bragging about how great you and your company are does not differentiate you from everyone else saying the same worn out lines.

There are some prospects that will make fast decisions based on your skilful diagnosis of your prospect's problems and goals. That is fine if your prospect decides to move fast. My only guidance is to make sure you do your due diligence in diagnosing, that way you don't commit sales malpractice.

Be awesome and take action with your prospects.

Here are the steps to this process:

Generate rapport and establish credibility

People do business with people they like and feel they can trust. Since you are looking to secure a new business client, your job is to make the customer want to do business with you on two levels, rationally and emotionally. To meet their emotional needs, you will have to make a favorable impression within the first thirty seconds. After making a favorable impression, focus your attention on listening intently and show genuine interest in them. Show lot's of enthusiasm.

Successful sales people establish rapport quickly with a prospect and adapt their approach based on the prospects personality type, not vice versa. If your customer is relaxed and low-key, be casual and low-key. If, your customer is strictly business and in a hurry, eliminate the small talk and cut to the chase. If they are passionate about their business or hobby or kids, go with the flow. Next, you need to adapt your approach to the situation and their personality type. Approaching everyone the same will not work.

Adapting your approach is generally two dimensional. The first factor is speed and pace. This is generally easy to gauge and should be evident before you meet with your client in person. The second factor is task and/or relationship oriented, which stems from their personality. If the person is left brained and makes decisions based primarily on information, establish your creditability and focus on your deliverables. If they are relationship oriented, show more interest in them and their business. Be interested, not interesting. Give them a soapbox to talk. Focus on their needs and listen intently.

Gather additional information

Now that you've established a common ground and created some mutual interest, it's time to gather up some information beyond what you've gleaned from your previous phone conversation.

During this process, you are trying to understand their key business issues, organizational structure, demonstrate areas that you can quickly add value or save money, complexity of the assignment, and their true objectives. During this exchange, focus on the benefits of your service and how it will help them.

Propose action and get them involved

The next hurdle in this process is to recommend solutions to the client's problems and concerns. Guide the prospect by focusing on the benefits that are most important to them. If you provide these benefits in a unique or proprietary way, emphasize this.

Gain agreement and secure a financial commitment

Once you secure their agreement to your proposal or services, stop selling and transition into execution mode. If you continue to focus on the selling, you may uncover an issue that you can not resolve and potentially lose the sale.

Some degree of financial commitment is important at the end of every sales transaction. If you haven't secured an agreement at the end of your meeting, secure a commitment to some course of action.

Selling and Dating Are the Same

If you can keep in mind that your goal is to attract and not to chase, you will find selling more enjoyable for both parties. You can also use this strategy in dating, but that is a topic for another day!

Here is a list of things to remember if you want to do both successfully!

- There is a fine line between persistence and stalking
- You have to kiss a lot of toads before you find your prince or princess

- There is no such thing as the perfect date
- You are more interesting when you are more interested in them
- Nothing good comes after the word, "but"
- Desperate people do desperate things
- Playing hard to get, works
- Nice people finish first

Epilogue

Michael Alexander is a highly successful sales executive and sales trainer and has over 25 years experience working with numerous Fortune 500 companies around the globe. His incredible sales success has been attributed to following a simple strategic plan and remaining highly motivated.

This unique book unveils proven, practical sales strategies that can be implemented quickly for immediate success and offers life changing motivational tips that will have you re-energized and ready to tackle your next sales call or re-focus your sales team.

It is designed for the on-the-go salesperson and sales manager and will not slow you down with long theory or case studies. These outstanding, unique tips will assist you in making your selling careers even more successful.

Whether you are selling B2B or B2C, you will want to continually reference this book to help keep you motivated on your journey to sales success.

www.ingramcontent.com/pod-product-compliance
Lightning Source LLC
Chambersburg PA
CBHW051313170526
45166CB00002B/528